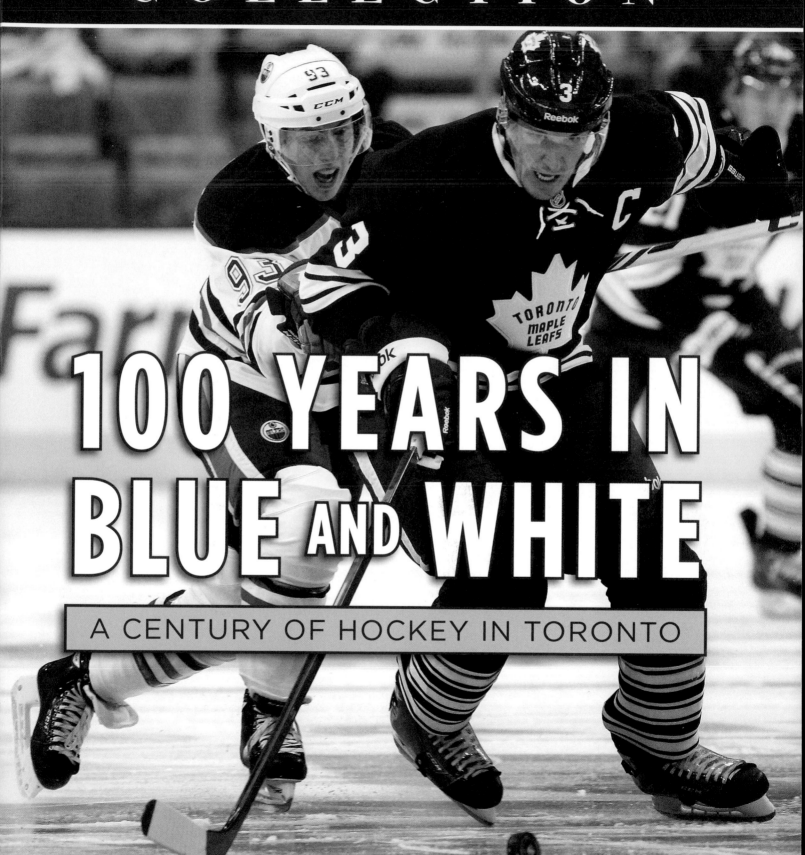

TORONTO ST[...]
COLLECTION

100 YEARS IN BLUE AND WHITE

A CENTURY OF HOCKEY IN TORONTO

Copyright © 2016 Toronto Star Newspapers Limited
No part of this publication may be reproduced, stored in a retrieval system, or transmitted in any form by
any means, electronic, mechanical, photocopying, or otherwise, without prior written permission of the publisher,
Triumph Books LLC, 814 North Franklin Street; Chicago, Illinois 60610 U.S.A.

This book is available in quantity at special discounts for your group
or organization.For further information, contact:

Triumph Books LLC
814 North Franklin Street
Chicago, Illinois 60610 U.S.A.
Phone: (312) 337-0747
www.triumphbooks.com

Printed in U.S.A.
ISBN: 978-1-62937-396-6

The Toronto Star
Edward A. MacLeod: COO Print
Ed Cassavoy: Director, Reader Engagement
& Content Commercialization—Print
Phil Bingley: Book editor
Carol Elder: Text and Visual Research

Includes content previously published by The Toronto Star

Design by Mojo Media, Inc.
Page production by Alex Lubertozzi

Opposite page photo by Lucas Oleniuk/Toronto Star
Front cover photos by USA TODAY Sports Images (Mats Sundin) and AP Images (background)
Back cover photo by AP Images

CONTENTS

1917-1927

The Beginning

The Maple Leafs actually begin life as the Montreal Canadiens before morphing into the Toronto Blueshirts, then the Arenas, later the St. Patricks and finally the team we know today.

FAST FACTS

- The National Hockey League comes into being on November 26, 1917 and begins to compete for the Stanley Cup.

- The Toronto Arenas, a charter member of the NHL, win 13 of 22 regular season games in 1917-18, then go on to win the Stanley Cup.

- The Arenas are renamed the Toronto St. Patricks before the 1919-20 season. The St. Pats finish with a 12-12 record and miss the playoffs.

- Cecil "Babe" Dye signs with the St. Patricks in December 1919 and scores 11 goals in 23 games in his first season. He then leads the team in scoring for the next five seasons.

- John Ross Roach takes over in goal in 1921 and leads the St. Patricks to their first and only Stanley Cup victory in March 1922.

- Foster Hewitt does first radio broadcast of a hockey game on March 22, 1923—a senior game between Kitchener and Toronto Parkdale—on Canada Covers America First, a radio station owned by the Toronto Star.

- Clarence "Hap" Day is signed in 1924 by the St. Pats. He is named captain of the Maple Leafs in 1927 and plays 14 seasons in Toronto. Day is then hired as the Leafs coach in 1940, winning five Stanley Cup championships in the next 10 years.

- Ace Bailey joins the team for the 1926-27 season and leads the St. Patricks with 28 points in 42 games.

- New owners led by Conn Smythe pay $160,000 for the St. Patricks in January 1927 and announce that they will rename the team The Toronto Maple Leaf Hockey Club Limited.

Ace Bailey led the Toronto St. Pats in scoring in 1926-27 with 28 points in 42 games. (Nat Turofsky/HHOF Images)

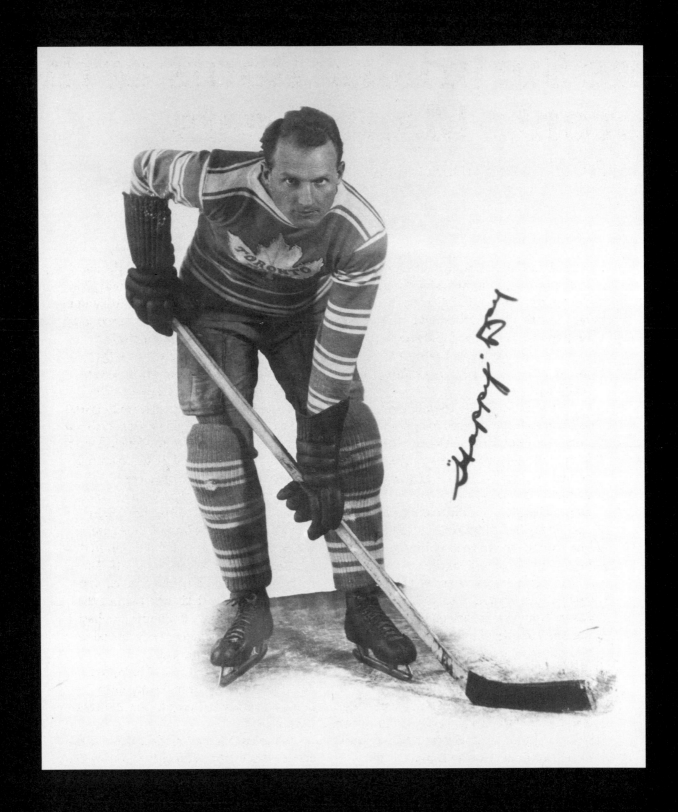

The Surprising Roots of the Toronto Maple Leafs

By Jim Proudfoot • Published: December 8, 1990

An absolutely astounding piece of historical information has just come to light. You're going to find it difficult to believe but its authenticity is beyond question. So prepare to be amazed, and then read on.

The Toronto Maple Leafs started life as the Montreal Canadiens. No kidding. They really did.

Now the Montreal-Toronto rivalry isn't as bitter as before. It used to be a feud like no other in the National Hockey League. We're talking bloodshed here, folks. But enough excitement is left to create a lively demand for tickets to next Wednesday's game at Maple Leaf Gardens, the Canadiens against the Buds. This remains the matchup local connoisseurs ache to witness, hoping for a return of the old magic.

Under the circumstances, then, it's really a gem authors Joseph Romain and James Duplacey unearthed in researching *The Toronto Maple Leafs: Images of Glory*, their handsomely illustrated tale of the franchise.

The Montreal Canadiens were charter members of the National Hockey Association, which was formed in 1909 and would exist for eight winters before becoming the National Hockey League. After that initial season, the NHA heard from a gentleman named George Kennedy. He owned what was called the Club Athletique Canadien in Montreal and was threatening the NHA with legal action for stealing a name that belonged to him, officially.

He was offering a way out, however. He'd call off his attorneys, he said, if he were licensed to operate a team in the NHA. So the struggling Haileybury, Ont., club was uprooted and transferred to Montreal where Kennedy was installed as owner. Naturally, he called his outfit Les Canadiens.

Meanwhile, the original 1909–10 Canadiens were sold to Toronto people, who waited until the Mutual St. Arena was completed in 1912 and then entered NHA competition as the Blueshirts. The Blueshirts later became the Arenas, who became the St. Patricks, who became the Maple Leafs in 1927 after being purchased by the late Conn Smythe. They moved to their present home in 1931.

But it's clear the Leafs of today are descended directly from the organization that came into being as the Montreal Canadiens.

"Charles Coleman made a vague reference to this in *The Trail of the Stanley Cup*,

Hap Day played 14 seasons for Toronto before taking over as the Leafs coach in 1940. (Nat Turofsky/HHOF Images)

"The Blueshirts managed to assemble five athletes who would eventually be enshrined in the Hall of Fame: Frank Nighbor, Harry Holmes, Frank Foyston, Jack Marshall and Harry Cameron."

which is the main source for any history of hockey," says Joe Romain. "We realized it would be important in any history of the Leafs. So we did some more digging."

Simultaneously, York professor Frank Cosentino was preparing The Renfrew Millionaires and from different archives altogether, made the identical discovery. The Millionaires also played in that first league, which is why the strange birth of the Leafs came to his attention.

The Blueshirts would have been contenders immediately if they'd inherited the Canadiens' players with the franchise. Among them were Jean Baptiste Laviolette and Didier Pitre, two of the most talented Francophones ever to wear skates. But NHA rules didn't allow them to leave Quebec.

Still, the Blueshirts managed to assemble five athletes who would eventually be enshrined in the Hall of Fame: Frank Nighbor, Harry Holmes, Frank Foyston, Jack Marshall and Harry Cameron. With a few changes, they won the Stanley Cup in 1914.

Eddie Livingston, who already owned the Toronto Tecumsehs, purchased the Blueshirts in 1915 and merged them as the Arenas when the league wouldn't let him run two teams. Despite winning the newborn

NHL's first Stanley Cup championship in 1918, the Arenas folded with two games to go a year later. The proprietors started over again that autumn as the St. Patricks and were rewarded with another Stanley Cup three years later. Smythe took over and changed the name, the colors and the logo in keeping with an intense patriotism, which would never waver.

If only for the wonderful old photos, *Images of Glory* is worth its enormous ($29.95) price. But the yarns are terrific, too. For example, Romain and Duplacey tell about a game at Mutual St. in 1926 when the St. Pats' Babe Dye lost his temper, seized the only puck in the building and sulkily refused to give it back to referee Bobby Hewitson. He remained adamant despite pleas from his teammates, the opposition and the spectators, of course. Finally, Hewitson cancelled the game and awarded it to the visitors—the Montreal Canadiens, naturally. ●

Editor's note: *The Toronto Maple Leafs: Images of Glory* **by James Duplacey and Joseph Romain was published by Canada McGraw-Hill Ryerson, Limited in 1990.**

Dennenay Sparks Arenas' Sensational Cup Victory

Published: April 1, 1918

That the Stanley Cup sojourns in Toronto and not in Vancouver for the summer months, is due to a blue-clad player about the size of a pint of cider or a 30-second minute—Corbett Dennenay, the Cornwall boy who has been Torontos' "pinch hitter" for a couple of seasons.

Young Dennenay, who has everything that goes to make up a star pro player but size, came through with the goal tht won the cup series for Toronto within nine minutes of the completion of the hour's play in the final game of the series at the Arena Saturday night.

It was a sensational goal, in a sensational game, and to say that the crowd enthused over young Dennenay and the winning goal is putting it mildly.

For 41 minutes the rival teams had battled grimly, determinedly, cleanly and scorelessly. Then the rotund Alfie Skinner, who had been chasing that lil' old puck all over the ice heap and pestering the life out of every opponent who laid a stick on it, sailed down the right boards and heaved a 60-foot lob at Goalkeeper Lehmann.

It looked as easy to handle as a couple of fresh eggs in a glass. In fact, it was too easy. Lehmann missed it, and Alfred did a hula-hula down the ice and tried to kiss the bald spot on Cyclone Taylor's head, while the crowd yelled itself to a whisper.

After 41 minutes of scoreless hockey that one goal loomed up as large as an elephant at a tea party. It was as welcome as whiskey at an Irish wake. Both goalkeepers had been doing such marvellous work and both defences had been so steadily effective that it looked as if that one goal would win the silverware, but the Vancouvers had courage to burn.

They came on steadily, and after being foiled a dozen times when goals looked likely in the next nine minutes, finally landed the tying counter. "Cy" Taylor notched the tally on a pass from "Tornado" McKay.

Then the fat was in the fire in real earnest. Both sides buckled into the fray with every last ounce of speed, courage and determination and the crowd rocked with excitement.

When things were in the balance in the previous two periods Dennenay had been showing some sensational hockey, and so when things were in extremes to the little slender Cornwall lad the crowd looked for the game's salvation.

He had made some wonderful efforts to wiggle through the three and four-man defence Vancouver had been employing all evening, and, in spite of the fact that he had been bumped over and tripped every time he had come down and he had been inside and missed one or two counters by inches, he was still trying with every ounce he had.

Dennenay had the crowd with him every time he tried a rush. To land the winning goal he brought the puck from mid-ice alone, side-stepped and out-guessed four men en route and, standing on one foot, dodged goalkeeper Lehmann's plunge and slide at him, and flipped the puck in. He was so far overbalanced that he clashed into the goal post before he could pull up.

The remaining six minutes were tense with excitement. The Millionaires threw everybody but Lehmann and one defence man up on the attack and strove valiantly to tie up, but the Arenas fastened to the puck-carriers like bull pups to ham bones, and they seldom got a decent shot.

The Arenas tightened up to a four-man defence and delayed the game every way they could. Three times they were called for playing "rag" behind the nets.

It was a good hard game all the way and it was superbly handled by the best pair of officials in the business, Harvey Pulford of Ottawa and Russell Bowie of Montreal. They made no mistakes, and they dropped on anything that looked like roughness with "a dull sickening thud."

There was only one penalty in the first period—"Cy" Taylor for loafing—but in the second and third the referees rode the players to the clink so assiduously that three times during the evening Toronto found their two subs used up and Vancouver was forced to drop a man and equalize the sides at five men each.

Outside of a jab Skinner took at Cook's head after the latter had mussed him up behind the nets there wasn't a thing that looked at all crude. The other penalties were all for slashes, trips or hard bodychecks into the boards.

Outside of Dennenay's great work, the outstanding feature was the marvellous work of Harry Holmes and Hugh Lehmann, the rival goalkeepers. No better exhibition of goal-guarding has ever been seen in Toronto than this pair gave Saturday night. They were both wizards.

It was positively uncanny the way in which this pair came out and out-guessed players who had penetrated the defences. The crowd cheered them time and time again.

Everybody else played well. Skinner's backchecking and tireless energy, which featured every game of the series, again made him stand out on Torontos' forward line, but Noble and Randall did great work. Cameron made some spectacular rushes and Mummery was a second goalkeeper. He stopped as many shots as Holmes did.

For Vancouver, McKay played a sensational game and Taylor had the crowd cheering him like a home-town favorite. Lloyd Cook and the rest of them were right at the top of their form and worked so hard and gamely that they had half the crowd cheering them.

In fact the truth is that Vancouver plainly outplayed Toronto in the first chapter, so much so that the odds dropped from 2 to 1 on Torontos down to 6 to 5, and they also had enough margin in the second period to force the "odds to evens."

In the final period, the Arenas, who had faded in earlier games in the series, came on, and showing unexpected stamina, had a margin in the play.

The game might well have ended in a tie as Skinner's goal, beautifully placed and all as it was, must be regarded as somewhat lucky.

Everything else from long range that came Lehmann's way he handled with careless ease. How he managed to miss the Skinner shot is the mystery of the game. ●

When Toronto Eyes Were Smilin'

On March 17, 1922—St. Patrick's Day—the Toronto St. Pats, forerunners to today's Maple Leafs, began the best-of-five Stanley Cup final against the Vancouver Millionaires. They lost that game 4–3, but St. Pat fans continued to pack the Arena Gardens in Toronto, where the series went the limit, with the St. Pats winning their first and only Cup. The following is an excerpt from the colorful report filed by the legendary Lou Marsh on the March 28 game that cinched the Cup.

By Lou Marsh • Published: March 28, 1922

Just cancel that order for the town band and tell the mayor of Vancouver he needn't sit up any more composing his ode of "Welcome to the Victorious Warriors." There ain't going to be no welcome for the Pacific coast champions in the city by the western ocean. The Millionaires are going home labeled "Thirty Cents," and the Stanley Cup will remain here in Toronto with the once-despised St. Patricks team. The Millionaires team turned out like an auction room watch—looks well, but won't stand the wear and tear.

The Irish squad just whaled the Coasters 5–1 last night in the deciding game and what is more, they looked that much the better team, and the sharks who laid in their toad skins at 8 to 5 and 2 to 1 turned out to be just plain gold fish. The pikers gathered all the gravy. The result was absolutely the biggest surprise of the upsettingist hockey season we ever had in this chunk of the old hemisphere.

The ragged-looking battlers in the green shirts hopped right into the silver-ware scramble with the bell, and proceeded to show the boys from the foggy western coast that they were much the best team, even without Eddie Gerard, the defence-man they borrowed from Ottawa to help them out Saturday night. (Harry) Cameron went back to his old place on the defence and "crippled" around like a 2-year-old. Any old time the management wants Cammy to star they should hamstring him. He goes better when he is wounded. He was one of the stars of an all-star team. Ken Randall, the other cripple—the most useful player St. Pats had all through the season—sat on the bench and saw the man who relieved him, Rod Smylie, step out and play sensational hockey. On the last

That must prove either one of two things—that Roach is a net wizard and (Hugh) Lehman just ordinary, or that St. Pats are wonderful snipers and that the Vancs were shooting like old women.

games the dashing dentist has cinched a regular berth on St. Pats, 1923.

St. Pats did not win because they had the breaks. They won because they were the better team and they played the best hockey from end to end.

The Westerners played like a telegraph message all through the piece—in dots and dashes. They couldn't get anywhere simply because they were checked off their feet. Their shooting was atrocious all through the piece. They were checked so assiduously that they hadn't much time to get their elbows rested or their sights adjusted.

Can you imagine that for a professional champion team—31 shots without a single score. In the final session when the protégés of the snake-chasing saint were sitting tight with everybody doing duty in the second and third line trenches they heaved 21 at (John Ross) Roach and only one got by, while the Irish got two counters on 12 shots.

That must prove either one of two things—that Roach is a net wizard and (Hugh) Lehman just ordinary, or that St. Pats are wonderful snipers and that the Vancs were shooting like old women.

Personally, I think that it was just a little of both.

The Vancouver team is the heavier and stronger team and they had the edge in speed, possibly not man to man, but in the aggregate, but the Irish squad showed that they had the brains, the pep, and the heart when it came to the pinch, and they trounced them thoroughly.

Babe Dye laid that old black bun on the target with terrific speed all night and scored four of the five goals. When he whipped it in it almost whined like a ricocheting bullet.

The defence work of (Bill) Stuart and Cameron was by far their best this season, but both excelled themselves offensively.

The boy with the sunset hair rushed incessantly. He carried the puck well, took advantage of the openings and had a keen ear out for pass signals.

He could have stuffed his lugs with cotton batten and heard Almighty Voice Dye.

He handed the Grand Llama of the Kingdom of Shoot two great across-the-ice passes and his nobs laid the ebony tablet on the altar of victory. ●

Babe Dye scored four goals as the St. Pats beat Vancouver 5-1 to win the 1922 Stanley Cup. (Nat Turofsky/HHOF Images)

Leafs' First Cup and a New Home

Conn Smythe takes control as the Leafs win their first Stanley Cup, Maple Leaf Gardens opens, the "Kid Line" soars and Ace Bailey barely survives a beating at the hands of Boston's Eddie Shore.

FAST FACTS

- Ace Bailey scores twice on Feb. 17, 1927 as the newly-re-named Maple Leafs win their first NHL game, 4-2 over the New York Rangers.

- Conn Smythe takes over as coach and general manager on the Maple Leafs to begin the 1927–28 season.

- Hap Day is named captain of the Leafs in November 1927, a job he will hold for 10 years.

- Toronto Star sports editor Lou Marsh reports in February 1928 that while professional hockey is played in New York on Sunday nights, "It is against the law to broadcast it."

- Charlie Conacher scores a goal in his first game as a Maple Leaf on Nov. 14, 1929. He and his "Kid Line" teammates Joe Primeau and Harvey "Busher" Jackson proceed to lead the team in scoring for the next seven seasons.

- Lieut. Governor W.D. Ross lays the cornerstone at Maple Leaf Gardens as a large crowd watches on September 21, 1931.

- Ken Doraty scores at 4:46 of the sixth overtime period on April 4, 1933 as the Maple Leafs defeat Boston 1-0 to win the fifth and deciding game of the Stanley Cup semi-finals. Leafs lose in the finals to New York.

- Syl Apps leads the Leafs in scoring in 1936–37 with 45 point in 48 games and wins the Calder Trophy as the NHL's outstanding rookie.

- Goalie Walter "Turk" Broda is purchased from the Detroit Red Wings in 1936 for $7,500. He goes on to win six Stanley Cups, the most by any goaltender in Leafs history.

- Coach Dick Irvin, who led the Leafs to their first Stanley Cup win in 1932, leaves Toronto in 1940 to take over as coach of the arch-rival Montreal Canadiens.

Maple Leafs Gardens was home to the Leafs from 1931 until 1999. (Bob Olsen/Toronto Star)

Brilliant Victory for Maple Leafs

Change of Management and Uniforms Appears to Have Chased the Jinx

By Bob Hayes • Published: February 18, 1927

Has the jinx gone?

The St. Patrick's, pardon me. Maple Leafs, appear to think so, as last night they put the New York Americans to rout and won 4–1. This knocked the Americans out of the third hole though it did not better the standing of the local club.

Well, how was it done?

In the first place the players had on a new uniform (they looked like a lot of galloping ghosts in white), they had a new coach, a new management and a new player.

The new coach, Alex Romeril, put Happy Day back on the defence and the changed worked wonders. Day made his reputation as a defense player when he was with Varsity and Hamilton Tigers but has always been used on the forward line by the St. Pats. He worked well last night and will soon be just as good as ever.

The new player was Carl Voss, who signed a contract late yesterday afternoon. Voss was a member of the Kingston junior champions last year and played with Marlboros this season. He is a husky defence player but appeared a little nervous last night. Given the chance he should make good.

Last night's game was one of the best, if not the best, of the season. All of the Leafs played hard and there was very little illegal work.

The game opened fast and within five minutes of the start the visitors were one goal ahead.

They staged an attack and J.R. Roach stopped a shot and a rebound, clearing the latter into a corner, where Lionel Conacher was camped. He passed out to Billy Burch, who was uncovered in front and scored.

This was the only tally for the New Yorkers as the Irish looked best for the balance of the period, but were unable to get the puck into the net.

With half of the second period gone, Bill Brydge staged a nice little rush, passed the puck to George Patterson who tied the count with a lovely goal.

Four seconds before the close of the period Bert Corbeau made a rush and Leo Reise played the man instead of the puck. He missed both and Corbeau passed out to Ace Bailey who put the locals in front.

The final period had the crowd on its feet all the time and both Roach and Forbes had to

do some tall stepping to keep their charges clear. After nearly sixteen minutes' play Bailey broke through and going down the centre put the game on ice with a lovely shot.

This was not to be the last goal, however, as just 15 seconds later Bailey and Corbeau made a dash together with the latter ending the rush by putting the puck into the net for his first goal of the season.

The Americans put all they had into the game, but could not outguess the plays of the local team.

Conacher put in a wonderful game for the losers. He was brilliant in many rushes, and played a wonderful defence game.

Burch was good on the forward line but the teamwork of the Irish defence kept him from scoring after the opening period.

The pleasing feature of the game was the wonderful showing of Corbeau on the defence. He worked harder than at any other time this season and was very effective.

Bill Carson was only used in spots and though his injured shoulder still affected him he did some good work.

Bailey worked at centre ice, and turned in his best game for some weeks. He scored two counters, and also had an assist besides giving the American defence plenty of trouble throughout the game.

Patterson and Butch Keeling also did some useful work and showed that they were not afraid to step in and take the bumps if necessary.

If the locals play the same kind of a game at the Arena tomorrow against the Montreal Maroons then it is sure that another victory will be chalked up.

Last night's was the first victory of the Toronto team against one of the teams in its own section of the league. ●

Bill Carson helped the Maple Leafs to their first win on February 17, 1927 despite a shoulder injury.
(Nat Turofsky/HHOF Images)

Leafs Win Three Straight and Capture Stanley Cup

New York Rangers Bow to Toronto after Great Hockey Display

By Lou Marsh • Published: April 11, 1932

Can you imagine it? Three in a row from Rangers!

New York!

There is the unmistakable answer to the slimy insinuations of the Slippery Sams who insidiously sent it out over the "grapevine route" that the Maple Leafs would toss off Saturday night's third Stanley Cup game for the sake of two more big gates for the Gardens and their club.

And what a lacing the Leafs gave Colonel Hammond's Hussars in their emphatic answer to the murderous attack upon the integrity of professional hockey.

Fourteen thousand three hundred and sixty-six paying guests packed the Carlton St. Palais de Glace and went early into a general and sustained mob hysteria as the Leafs larruped the newly-crowned league champions 6–4 and won the Stanley Cup in the grand finale of the greatest hockey season Toronto ever experienced.

And that goes three ways—cash, crowd, and competition—amateur as well as pro.

The score by periods tells the bald tale of Leafs' convincing superiority—2–0–3–1—6–4.

Add that 6–4 and the 6–4 score at New York and the 6–2 win at Boston and let the significance of those three convincing wins

sink home—18 goals to 10—surely convincing evidence of the Leafs' complete mastery of the league champions.

There never was a moment when the issue was in doubt—never a second when that mob of hockey-mad fanatics doubted the integrity of the team or its ability to trounce the Patrickmen.

The Flying Frenchmen?

Don't ever talk about the Flying Frenchmen in the same breath as the Toronto Tornados after Saturday night's exhibition of sustained speed, courage, endurance and strategy. Saturday night's torrent of speed would have left even the cyclonic Canadiens hogtied and helpless.

Stop me if you have heard this before—no team you ever saw would have beaten those Leafs Saturday night!

They were a team—a real team. Every man jack was in there and starring—doing his bit plus.

They had to be, for Bill Cook and his battlers fought it out like cornered bobcats—fought until they sagged at the knees and had merry-go-rounds in their heads. They didn't quit. Just when it looked as if human endurance was at an end back they came to turn what looked like a rout into rugged battling and more or less close finish.

The Rangers were actually forcing the pace the last five minutes.

Give them credit, boys.

They were as magnificent in defeat as the Leafs were in victory.

Lester Patrick tried everything in a hockey general's repertoire to stem the avalanche of speed. His big, burly defence men hurled themselves into the Leaf forwards relentlessly and his forwards not only tried to match speed with speed but crashed into the Leafs' stonewall defence as recklessly as dervishes crashed Gordon's squares of British redcoats.

The Leafs set the pace and the Rangers followed them.

The New York squad asked no quarter and gave none, and when it was all over made no excuses. They were beaten by a better team—and they admitted it like true sportsmen—but they did not admit defeat until the last bitter second had expired. The Rangers are a team of gamesters.

And the crowd acknowledged their keen, rugged, plucky effort by cheering them to the echo as they fraternized with the joy-mad Leafs and together—victor and vanquished—they dragged their weary, battered bodies to the showers.

After all, why shouldn't the crowd cheer them?

Every man jack on the Ranger team except Desjardines is a Canadian.

The game itself was a brilliant exposition of hockey. Speed was the predominant factor. Every man stood up under the grueling, and both teams turned loose a bewildering display of beautifully timed combinations. There were no fluke goals. Every counter was earned by sheer wizardry of stick, blade and brain.

Individual heroes were as scarce in that battle as ant-eaters in Alaska. Everybody was a star at times—principally all the time.

The goal scoring gives no edge to any Leaf, particularly because every Toronto goal came on a combination, and only one man—Andy Blair—scored more than once. With Rangers it was a bit different. Frank Boucher, veteran centre ice wizard of the Patrickmen, scored three of Rangers' four goals and gave the assist to Bun Cook for the fourth. The Rangers' Musketeers—Cook, Boucher, and Cook—did all the scoring for the beaten team, a truly remarkable record when it is considered that the Rangers had three other complete lines, or nine forward s in all. The defence men, all of whom bulked hugely in the defeat of the Canadiens, did not figure on the score sheet at all, except in the bad boy column.

The skeleton of the battle is soon filled in for those who only want the highlights.

The Leafs stepped out like quarter horses—all hot and raring to go. They forced the early pace and had the fans on their feet roaring from the first drop of the puck. The first break came when he threatened Depot de Chabot.

With the puck chasing pharmacist on the roost Leafs refused to let the Rangers take the play against them. They forced the pace. The crowd roared when Ott Heller, the Kitchener youngster on the Ranger defence, skied Cotton and got away with it. Clancy came right back with a spill for Heller his next trip down. Just as soon as Day got back he tore in on the Ranger nets and stirred things up like a bull terrier in a rabbit hutch.

Then came the Leafs' first goal. Blair nailed that off a sweet rush and pass by Clancy about five and a half minutes after the play started.

The crowd screamed and stamped and cheered, but before they had come back to normalcy Blair was back for another one. This one came from Gracie's best play of the night. North Bay Bob came down at top speed and he and Blair double passed. Gracie was hurled out of scoring range. He went in behind the nets, battled away for the puck, got it and after three attempts got it out to Blair who potted the pellet.

That set the crowd mad with delight. It showed them that Leafs were on the bit and that there would be no gate-grabbing shenanigan. From then on the tension was relieved and the fans settled back to enjoy the incidents of a contest that always looked to be labeled for the Leafs.

For the rest of the period the play seesawed but the Leafs were always on top even when they were short-handed through penalties.

Harvey Jackson

The outstanding incident of the latter part of the period was a major penalty to Jackson for bouncing his club—off Ching Johnson's head. Referee Mallinson gave the penalty and the crowd howled the well-known "murder."

They could not see why Jackson should get more than two minutes because he did not draw blood.

If he didn't draw blood he raised an egg.

In the second period the battle was even and the pace still hot. For a while it looked as if the Rangers might still be dangerous, but the pace finally told on the New York squad and the growing tension was relieved when a beautifully timed three way combination of the Kid Line gave Jackson his only goal of the

night. That was just after the ten minute mark. That made it 3–0.

Five minutes later the Rangers showed that they were still in the battle by sinking home the puck after a Heller to Boucher combination.

Even with the score 3 to 1 the Leafs did not look to be in trouble or danger.

The period almost ended in tragedy.

In the last two minutes of play young Chuck Conacher, 205 pounds of TNT, let one of his smoke shots go from away over by the fence just inside the blue line.

Roach, as game as a badger, threw himself in front of the sizzler and it hit him under the heart. The terrific impact drove him back into the nets, but he straightened up again and the puck was cleared.

Then he slowly dropped his stick, struggled a second with his gloved hands at his throat, and silently folded up and dropped to the ice.

He looked like a man shot through the heart.

There was a moment's awed silence and then a rippling groan as Roach stiffened out on the ice. It looked as if the popular little Port Perry netman had been killed, for he lay without a move.

It was a solar-plexus blow—a shock to the big motor centre of the body. It took Roach five minutes to recover. But it didn't break his nerve.

He was even better than ever after the knockout.

Halfway down the third period the Leafs rammed home two more goals. Finnigan and Day and Bailey on a three-way combination with Conacher and Day, and that settled the issue beyond a doubt.

After that the Leafs just held them.

With five minutes to go Bun Cook got Rangers' second goal and caused a flurry, but when Gracie and Finnigan came back with their goal a minute later the crowd settled back satisfied.

The Rangers got the last two goals in jigtime—1.04 and 50 seconds—both on sparkling plays by Boucher, but they were too far back to really threaten the Leafs' lead.

It was a wide-open game—a game that would have been a wow even if the Stanley Cup had not depended upon it.

It was possibly the best all-round game of the local season. ●

Busher Jackson had five goals in seven playoff games as the Leafs won the 1932 Stanley Cup. (Nat Turofsky/HHOF Images)

Remembering Ace Bailey and the True Birth of Leafs Nation

Leaf Star's Fight for Life Riveted and Galvanized a City

By Brendan Kennedy • Published: December 12, 2013

Eighty years ago today, Ace Bailey was nearly killed and Leafs Nation was born.

Sure, the foundation of frenzied fandom in this hockey-crazed city had already been built by national radio broadcasts in the 1920s, the opening of Maple Leaf Gardens in 1931 and the Leafs winning their first Stanley Cup—of the post-St. Pats/Arenas era—just five months later.

But the emotional rallying point that galvanized Toronto around its beloved Blue and White occurred in a game between the Leafs and Bruins at Boston Garden on Dec. 12, 1933, and in the tense days that followed, when Bailey's life hung in the balance.

During the game, Bailey, a longtime and well-liked Leaf who once led the league in scoring, was decked from behind by Boston's Eddie Shore so violently that Bailey landed headfirst, fracturing his skull and leaving him convulsing on the ice.

Bailey's condition was so dire that a priest was brought in to read the last rites, while newspaper editors prepared obituaries.

"Ace Bailey in Grave Condition After Hockey Clash," read the front page of the Toronto Daily Star on Dec. 14.

The paper also led with the story the morning after the game, but focused then on what seemed like the more pressing matter at the time: the arrest of Leafs general manager Conn Smythe, who was charged with assault after slugging a Bruins' fan in the midst of the melee.

"If I hit anyone, it was only in self-defence," Smythe said.

Meanwhile, Bailey was clinging to life.

In addition to the skull fracture, he suffered a cerebral hemorrhage and remained unconscious in a Boston hospital as doctors worked to relieve pressure on his brain.

"Physical Reserve Alone is Keeping Ace Bailey Alive," read another front-page headline in the Star on Dec. 14.

Bailey's struggle captivated the city, while a palpable outrage grew.

"Toronto fans are boiling over," wrote the Star's sports editor Lou Marsh in a front-page editorial.

"Half frantic, most of them who telephone in breathe threats of vengeance."

False rumours of Bailey's death also filtered through the city, sending "a wave of bitter resentment across the town."

Torontonians turned to the Star for verification, according to a story published Dec. 15 under the headline, "Star's switchboard fairly blazes with calls about Ace."

Word also spread that Bailey's father had boarded a train bound for Boston with a revolver and plans to kill Shore.

Facts are sparse on this bit of gossip—it may have been completely fabricated—but there are some reports from the time that Boston police caught wind of the elder Bailey's plans and managed to calm him.

What is certain is that Bailey's fight for survival was the biggest story in the city and perhaps the country, as hockey fans desperately sought news on the winger's well-being." Marsh wrote, adding in a separate editorial that Bailey's "courageous fight" had "roused the Canadian sporting world as no other tragedy."

Bailey remained front-page news for more than a week, while the Star had a reporter camped outside his hospital room giving readers a roller coaster of updates.

"'I feel fine,' says Bailey, out of coma" read a banner headline on Dec. 16. The subhead: "Injured player asks for drink of orange juice."

But the citrus celebrations were short-lived, as Bailey fell back into a coma and subsequent headlines despaired:

"Irvin 'Ace' Bailey maintains slight gain"

"Bailey still fighting valiantly for his life, odds seem hopeless"

"Public tension has grown to such a pitch regarding Bailey that it is almost hysterical," wrote Star sportswriter Alexandrine Gibb, who kept vigil outside Bailey's room.

"It has made us all forget that Christmas is just around the corner. For what is Christmas if Ace doesn't recover?"

"People were aghast," says hockey historian Kevin Shea, describing the mood in the city at the time. "(Bailey) had been a longtime fixture in town and all of a sudden here he is hit by one of the dirtiest players in the league....There was definitely real furor at the time."

From that furor grew unity—a common hope and shared grudge, the likes of which hadn't existed within the city's sports scene.

Doctors were at first doubtful Bailey would come out alive, calling the fact he had survived even a few days "a miracle."

Meanwhile, the Star's Gibb was painting a grim picture inside Bailey's hospital room: "The Boston City hospital in the silent Christmas night hours is, each night, the scene of a terrific struggle for life."

Then, 10 days after the hit, the first bit of positive news.

"Ace definitely recovering but may never play again," read the Star's front page.

"On a white cot in an ether-permeated room at the Boston City hospital, a miracle has apparently been accomplished," the story reads.

"Irvin 'Ace' Bailey, Toronto hockey star, who, by all the tenets of medical science should have been dead days ago, is definitely on the road to recovery."

"I knew the 'Ace' would never give up," Smythe, the Leafs' firebrand owner, said at the time. "I told you I'd bet on him against the opinion of the doctors."

Bailey survived, but true to the prognostications of the time, he never played again. It was another month before he was well enough to return to Toronto, where he was greeted at Sunnyside Station by fans.

The incident wasn't only seminal for the burgeoning Leafs Nation.

It also led many players to don head protection for the first time, while a benefit game—held for Bailey the following February—is considered the precursor to the modern all-star game.

Bailey, who died in 1992 after suffering a stroke, was inducted into the Hockey Hall of Fame in 1975 and is one of just two Leafs to have his number retired.

Shore, also considered one of the game's greats, was apparently angered after he was knocked down by popular Leafs brute, Red Horner.

The fact these two men were also involved in the incident made it even more compelling, Shea says.

"Shore wasn't hated, but he was certainly one of those guys that everybody's eyes were on when he came to town," Shea said.

Boston police questioned Shore but chose not to lay criminal charges.

Horner himself described the scene to a Star reporter the day after it happened.

"I looked down on the writhing form of Ace Bailey, who is like a brother to me, and I went sick all over," he said.

"The Ace had an expression on his face I will never forget. His mouth was hanging wide and his tongue was lolling. He was practically blue in the face, and my only thought was that Shore had pulled the dirtiest trick I had witnessed in my five years with the Maple Leafs. I feared Bailey might die."

Horner said he skated over to Shore and told him "in no mistakable terms" what he thought of him.

Shore didn't respond.

"He just stood there with a vacant expression on his face. So I repeated my statement and with that let him have it smack on the button. Sticks never entered the argument. My fist shows how he was hit."

On Jan. 4, 1934, in his first interview following the incident—conducted from his hospital bed—Bailey absolved Shore of blame, saying he believed the pair simply collided.

Though he told a different story 55 years later.

"I'll never forget it," he told the Star's Paul Hunter in 1988.

"You know, I'm sure Shore hit the wrong man. He mistook me for Red Horner."

Bailey explained that his teammate Horner had checked Shore into the boards and retrieved the puck, carrying it up the ice

as Bailey covered Horner's spot on the back end of the rush.

"As Shore turned to come back up ice he skated up behind me and he knocked my feet out from underneath me. My head hit the ice first and that was it. I was unconscious for 15 days." ●

Ace Bailey shook hands with Eddie Shore less than three month's after Shore's hit from behind ended Bailey's hockey career. (Nat Turofsky/HHOF Images)

Leafs and Miss Stanley Finally "Making Woo"

Schriner's Two Goals Put Snatch on Elusive Trophy

By Andy Lytle • Published: April 20, 1942

Shortly after ten-twenty on Saturday night before the greatest throng that ever looked at hockey final in the Dominion of Canada, Hap Day went flying over the ice.

He caught Schriner with one arm over this shoulder. His other fist Hap brought affectionately to Sweeney's cheek, playfully punched it.

"Hello champ," he greeted his left-winger.

"Champ yourself," retorted Sweeney.

A few seconds later Day had the Stanley Cup in his possession for the second time in his career. Ten long years he had helped in the win and oddly enough not a single player was left on the ice at these who had snatched it a decade ago.

We the crowd looked its frenzied fill Frank Calder presented the cup. There was a delay while captain Syl Apps skated over, one eye half closed and cut, yelled to Conn Smythe.

"Come on out Conn, you waited long enough for this cup. Come and get it."

Beaten in four straight games, the Red Wings went down with colors flying, eyes front and fighting doggedly to the last.

Syd Howe scored their only goal of the finale on a break-in with two of his mates. This came early in the second period.

Like a mother clings to her wayward son, the Wings held so tenaciously to the slim lead, fought so hard and checked so passionately, the third was a quarter gone before Schriner broke with Carr and Taylor shook the building to the girders as the immense crowd responded to this successful sally with a roar like the crashing of guns.

Schriner's goal was paved by a penalty to Orlando, who dumped Apps, dramatically cast gloves and stick to the ice, seized his head in both hands as he heard the whistle, saw Chadwick's upraised thumb.

Jimmy must be psychic, for that was the break the Leafs had to get to win. Jimmy was on the ice again but was still out of the play when Schriner jammed his goal home.

Leafs surged madly after this, played like men not to be denied their first clear unashamed look at the famous Stanley Cup.

It was Pete Langelle, snapping in a pass he had reached from Goldham and McCreedy, who turned the tide definitely in Leafs' favor.

Less than five minutes of play were left when Schriner went through again. In both his goals the play of Taylor and Carr bulked largely.

It was the "big line" of the team as hockey beat a belated retreat after a six months' stand.

There were 16,218 paid admissions. Add to that six or seven hundred complimentaries and the actual eye-witnesses to the climax of a tremendously hard fought and bitter series were close to 17,000, give or take the fractional customer, take it you are a gentleman who prefers brunettes.

Chadwick handed three two-minute penalties to McCaig, two to Orlando and one to Bruneteau. Leafs had Schriner, Davidson, Dickens and Nick Metz in the cooler.

In the type of game played by both teams in which the puck is hurled ahead and all hands chase it, penalties make little difference because it is all attack.

Twice when Leafs were short a man they threw the puck and chased it so stoutly Wings were constantly on defence.

Leafs outplayed the Wings in the first period were definitely running second in the next, scored all their goals in the third.

Chadwick's refereeing displeased some of the fans and they began to litter the ice with anything handy or good to throw. Papers came, the odd orange, assorted nuts, a light bulb and a large bottle opener.

But they stopped throwing anything but applause when Schriner and Langelle finally began dumping rubber behind the astute and brilliant Johnny Mowers.

Several of his stops in the early going were sensational. He robbed Apps, Schriner and Langelle of goals they figured to trickle in.

Though they had to lose finally, the Wings played bang-up hockey, attended strictly to the man with the puck.

It was a bitter pill they had to swallow because they had soared to the heights, were all ready to sip champagne from the Cup when it was snatched rudely from their lips in the fourth game.

But they went out like honorable men, beaten but not cowed. They gave way before a club that was good enough to readjust itself, play the enemy at its own game, out-score them at the wire.

Taking it four straight, the hard way, as the Leafs did, is something no team has ever done in the Stanley Cup stakes, hitherto. Bruins did it to Detroit, the easier way, last year. ●

Captain Syl Apps led the Leafs in scoring as they beat Detroit to win the 1942 Stanley Cup. (Nat Turofsky/HHOF Images)

Glory Years

Maple Leafs hit their stride, winning eight Stanley Cups with stars such as Turk Broda, Bill Barilko, Ted "Teeder" Kennedy, Max Bentley, Howie Meeker and eventually George Armstrong, Tim Horton, Johnny Bower, Dave Keon, Frank Mahovlich and Red Kelly.

FAST FACTS

- Howie Meeker scores 5 goals on Jan 8, 1947, setting an NHL rookie record, and goes on to win the Calder Trophy.

- Syl Apps leads the 1947–48 Leafs in scoring with 53 points in 55 games and then retires after the team wins the Stanley Cup.

- Joe Primeau, King Clancy, Howie Meeker and finally Bill Reay each take a turn behind the Leafs' bench but none succeeds in bringing home a championship.

- The seeds of future success are planted as future stars George Armstrong and Tim Horton (1952), Dick Duff and Billy Harris (1955), Bob Pulford (1956), Frank Mahovlich and Bob Baun (1957), Carl Brewer and Alan Stanley (1958) and Bob Nevin, Dave Keon and Eddie Shack (1960) are added to the roster.

- George Armstrong is appointed Leafs captain, a role he will fill for 11 seasons.

- General Manager George (Punch) Imlach fires coach Billy Reay in November 1958 and takes over behind the bench leading the Leafs into the playoffs for the first time in three years. Leafs overcome a 5-point deficit in the last three games of the regular season to qualify.

- Goaltender Johnny Bower is signed in 1959 after bouncing around the minor leagues for 13 years. The 35-year old rookie netminder helps Leafs qualify for the finals that season before winning the Stanley Cup in 1962, 1963, 1964 and 1967.

- All-Star defenceman Red Kelly is obtained from Detroit on February 10, 1960, in a trade for fringe player Marc Reaume. Kelly moves to centre and plays a key role in four Stanley Cup victories.

- Chicago Blackhawks co-owner James D. Norris offers the then-outrageous sum of $1 million in cash to purchase Frank Mahovlich outright from the Leafs. The offer is declined.

- Defenceman Bobby Baun scores the winning goal in overtime in Game 6 of 1964 Stanley Cup finals after suffering a broken ankle earlier in the game. He also plays in the Leafs' Cup-winning Game 7.

Toronto fans mobbed their heroes on Bay Street after the Leafs won 1963 Stanley Cup. (Frank Grant/Toronto Star)

Long Puck Harvest Ends with Leafs Triumphant

Babe Pratt's Third Period Goal Makes the Difference in Game 7

By Lewis Walter • Published: April 13, 1945

Toronto Maple Leafs are home with the Stanley Cup, and the puck-raggled Red Wings are left with memories of a great comeback that fell a mite short of the world hockey championship.

Babe Pratt, the big defenceman who was voted the Hart Trophy, the National Hockey League's most valuable player award, last season, proved last night that the award was a year early.

It was the petulant Babe, who started the winning play and finished it, to give the Leafs a 2–1 victory in the seventh and deciding game of the cup series last night.

A crowd of 14,890, largest ever to see a hockey game in Detroit, saw the Babe go to town with only eight minutes left, and with Syd Howe in the penalty box for high-sticking Gus Bodnar.

Pratt launched a long pass from the Detroit blueline to Nick Metz at the left of the Red Wings cage. As 18-year-old Harry Lumley made a sprawling save on the corner, Pratt came rushing up to jab the puck from under the goalie's pads and into the goal.

That last jab of Pratt's cut short one of the great comebacks in Red Wings history, Detroit was shut out in the first three games, 1–0, 2–0 and 1–0, then had rallied to take the next three including two on Toronto ice, by scores of 5–3, 2–0 and 1–0.

The Wings came into Olympia last night after a 1–0 overtime triumph in Toronto Saturday night. They felt the cup was almost within their grasp.

But Leafs made Wings hopes droop in the first period when Mel Hill took a pass from Ted Kennedy, slammed it to the far corner against an unprotected Lumley.

Capt. Bob Davidson had started the play with a drive down left wing and a shot which bounced around the net to Kennedy.

Expertly protecting their lead with the close defensive play which won the first three games, the Leafs held out until after eight minutes of the final period.

McCool had to make only one save in the second period. Capt. Flash Hollett split the defence of Morris and Pratt and lashed a 40-footer on which McCool made a diving save. He scrambled for the puck 12 feet

Babe Pratt poked in the winning goal as the Maple Leafs won the 1945 Stanley Cup. (Nat Turofsky/HHOF Images)

Fired by renewed prospects, the Wings flew in on a series of drives that brought McCool bustling out of his nets. A penalty to Howe spelled their doom, with Pratt scoring only 19 seconds after the Detroit veteran entered the box.

out on right wing. Murray Armstrong fished it back, then pitched it over the fallen goalie into an open net.

Fired by renewed prospects, the Wings flew in on a series of drives that brought McCool bustling out of his nets. A penalty to Howe spelled their doom, with Pratt scoring only 19 seconds after the Detroit veteran entered the box.

Penalties were even, with Referee Bill Chadwick calling two on each team in the close-checking game. He called the last one on Elwyn Morris of the Leafs for tripping Howe with 105 seconds left but the Detroit chance fizzled out after McCool kicked out hard shots by Liscombe and Armstrong.

Each goalie made 13 saves. By periods they were: McCool 5–1–7—13. Lumley 6–4–3—13.

As the last whistle sounded, Manager Jack Adams swung out on the ice where his Wings were congratulating their happy rivals. He walked over and shook hands with Coach Hap day, who met him half-way.

Then NHL President Mervyn Dutton presented the cup to the winners. Lieut. Com. Barry O'Brien, C.N. grandson of the donor, presented the O'Brien trophy to the runners-up.

Detroit played the last half of the game without Mud Bruneteau, put out of action when a slash on the shoulder numbed his left arm. There was no penalty, Bruneteau didn't even know who hit him.

Day used his third line of Art Jackson, Don and Nick Metz for only one turn in the first period. Metz was used regularly all the way here and there. ●

Leafs 'Ugly Ducklings' Hit the Jackpot

Comeback Sends Defending Champions Down to Defeat

By Joe Perlove • Published: April 21, 1947

There it is! The Stanley cup for the Toronto Maple Leafs!

They won it fair and square, too, with a come-from-behind 2–1 decision over the defending champions Montreal Canadiens in a wide open sixth game. And, in doing so, they left no doubt in the minds of close to 15,000 jubilant supporters as to their being worthy Cup holders.

Those ugly ducklings hit the jackpot! It's hard to believe that what was more or less a nondescript collection of sweaters and skates, a hope rather than a team, could in its first year as a unit reach the highest possible peak in the National Hockey League.

It must have been with many misgivings that club officials loosed this outfit from its cove back in October. It must have been with much shaking of heads they let these striplings out into the world where roamed such hardened hockey characters as the Canadiens, the Bruins, and the Red Wings.

The Leafian ship, which had sailed serenely these same waters for years and years, finally sprung a fatal leak last year, and had to be beached. And at a time when fresh material was conspicuous by its scarceness. The oldies had come to the end of the trail, but there was

no well prepared young ones crowding their footsteps in the hockey meat grinder.

Hugging the best of what was left, Conn Smythe and Hap Day shuffled through a flock of hopefuls and finally selected six they needed to make a quorum. But that's all it was, a quorum.

It wasn't to this season these two were looking. It wasn't even toward next season. They were just looking toward the future. How were they to know that this collection, the youngest hockey ship ever to be launched on such a tough journey, would outrace itself.

Youth being the exuberant commodity it is, the ship sailed jauntily, almost recklessly, into the fray. The youngsters didn't know from nothing except to play the hardest they could. They slammed into the opposition heedless of the known weaknesses of bone structures and heart and wing.

They flashed to the front and much to the surprise of seasoned observers, stubbornly stayed there. One and all expected them to subside, to come back to the field. They did come back a bit but not too far. Only the Canadiens, passed them in the 60-game long haul.

Just as youth is exuberant so is it unpredictable. Like a two-year old horse,

they'd occasionally forget about the job at hand, would stop to gawk at the crowd, shy at shadows, fail to answer the whip.

They surged and fell back through the playoffs. They sagged to the Red Wings and came smashing back to take three games straight. They sagged to the Canadiens and came back to even it up and take two more. They sagged again in the fifth game, but once again they came charging back, and this time it counted. This time they went over the top swamping the old champion en route.

Right off the bat in this final charge they were set on their heels. A bit of strategy backfired. Garth Boesch was moved over to Bill Barilko's left defence spot so that it would be he, and not the gauche Pacific Coast leaguer, who would be on the side Maurice Richard rockets in on.

On the first rush of the game, Buddy O'Connor swooped in and when Boesch moved to play him instead of the puck the little guy veered around him and zambo he scored! Many of the fans hadn't even reached their seats, were still stepping on toes, and falling over laps and here was that important first goal in the hands of the enemy.

The situation soon took a turn for the worse, for the Canadiens, riding that wave, swooped in again and again. But the Turkey, Broda was there, with sparks in his hair.

In the long run it looks as if the team went the way Broda went. When he was on, which he was most of the season, the team was winning. When he weakened, they weakened with him. He was their ace-in-the-hole in the playoffs. And he was strictly it Saturday night.

In the second period it was different. It was the Leafs' turn to surge. Apps, Watson and Ezinicki sparkled and tested the mighty Bill Durnan again and again. Teeder Kennedy, Vic Lynn and Howie Meeker uncorked some of their best efforts and there wasn't been much wrong with any of their efforts all season.

It was this line that tore it. Kennedy fought for the puck as ever. Meeker got a shot at it. Kennedy fought again and finally got it to Lynn and he hit with a screened shot to tie it up.

It was that trio that settled the issue finally with less than six minutes to play in the third. Again it was Kennedy who fought for possession and flicked it here and there to his mates till ready. Meeker got it out to him and it was over. ●

Montreal goaltender Bill Durnam stopped Syl Apps on this play but Maple Leafs prevailed 2-1 in Game 7 to win the Stanley Cup. (Nat Turofsky/HHOF Images)

Leafs 'Answered Every Question'

Sweep Red Wings to Capture Cup

By Joe Perlove • Published: April 15, 1948

Being as it's traditional in the newspaper racket to give the readers the sum and substance of the situation at the beginning it is hereby announced that the Maple Leafs today are Stanley cup winners for the second straight year.

They achieved that distinction, the first time in the history of the club that they've won this world's hockey title—discounting the possibility that Fujiama may have a great hockey team too—two years in a row, by blowing the Detroit Red Wings right tout of the contention by a 7 to 2 score before 14,043 fans last night.

All this foregoing may sound slightly disrespectful and heretical, but honest to goodness the few hairs I still do boast stood up, each and every one of them, when the organ ground out the Maple Leaf Forever, when the final bell rang.

Not because a Canadian team won it. That's so much eyewash. For after all how many non-Canadians are there in the league? It was mainly because this team has the goods, did the job, delivered the stuff, or call it what you may.

Folks, this is a hockey club and hardened as a sports writer gets watching one club after another, in any sport, he can't help but get a rise out of a good club.

So they'll tell you these guys would be murdered by say, the Rangers of Cooks, Boucher, Ching Johnston and such of '33 or the Kid Line, with Finnegan, Clancy, Day and Horner of '32, or the pre-war Bruins with the Kraut Line, Cowley, Crawford, Clapper and Brimsek.

Being of the "I'd have to see it" school, they'd have to show me the club that would whip this one. And that's taking into consideration that the league, like the old gray mare, ain't what she used to be.

Conn Smythe likes to say, at the slightest provocation, and as he said last night "this team answered every question." And that they did.

Don't forget that the top team in the league, as the Leafs were a year ago, gets the toughest competition. Everybody points for them. A team like Chicago on the other hand has it comparatively easy. Which could explain in part the fancy scoring feats of certain members of the Hawks under Chas. Conacher. They weren't on top with everyone shooting at them.

From the start once the Bostons started coming apart, it was obvious the Detroits were going to be stuffy about the gonfalon. Ups, downs, downs, ups and here they come down the stretch and the Detroits look to have it on the Leafs. Lumley is going to win the Vezina

trophy. The Wings are going to finish in front and grab off a thousand each.

So they stepped out and bashed the Wings two straight right on the wire, as if to say, "Look kids, fun's fun and all that, but don't get fresh."

Then down went the Bruins four to one and that one was by courtesy of "Mendel" attitude, and down went the mighty Wings the first three games. So maybe the Wings aren't a great team. It's still a feat of sorts to whip any club four straight.

That brings us to last night's encounter, and ruddy near time. The Detroits were desperate. Make no mistake about that. No starving brigand, putting the "heist" on a bank, was ever more aggressive.

They charged right into us (That's me, always with the winner) right from the start. Bang, smash and there's a penalty—to the Wings. Horeck tripped that nice Ezinicki. That was enough for us. There is an explosion. The puck caroms from here to there and Bentley, the skinny guy in the green hat, traps the puck at the line, slips it up through a knothole to Kennedy and it's in! All that in two minutes.

Being as it is a desperate encounter the Leafs contract a penalty. Metz, of all people, being so thoughtless as to trip. The Wings are blazing to get that goal back. In their hats. We get that goal back. Garth Boesch stops a puck that is shot straight at him by Jimmy Conacher,

breaks away, and though Conacher, one of the fastest skaters in the league is on his heels, he keeps ahead of him, rolls in on Lumley, and whango it's in again!

That's the current leafs for you. The opposition is shorthanded, the Leafs score. The Leafs are shorthanded, the Leafs score. That is a difficult situation to defeat. Or even tie.

Before the frame is over Harry Watson takes the puck when Syl Apps gets the draw on a face off and it's in. That Lumley. The higher the chips were piled up, the lower he went. With Broda it was the other way about.

Early in the third the McFadden-Pavelich-Horeck line presses against Kennedy et al, and Leo Reise scores. Aha, think the customers, here come the Wings now.

The Wings gang again and Thomson slips Syl Apps a break away pass and the cap is away and how. Lumley has no chance. Then Vic Lynn passes up to Kennedy in close and it's 5 to 1.

Lynn is off for interference and Watson gets a break away and it's in. In the third Bentley whirls up dekes Jack Stewart into the next county, passes to Costello, and it's in. Horeck from Fogolin, from a scramble closes the scoring. But the Leafs have taken four straight and in any league that's a first class accomplishment. ●

Goalie Turk Broda, Wally Stanowski and Howie Meeker teamed up to stop Detroit's Ted Lindsay as the Maple Leafs won the 1948 Stanley Cup. (Nat Turofsky/HHOF Images)

Toronto Makes It Three in a Row

By Joe Perlove • Published: April 18, 1949

After a number of years in this sports-writing business, one is inclined to acquire a jaundiced eye for everything connected with it. It gets so nothing is important, nothing is crucial.

Not even the winning of a Stanley cup by the home team. Not even when that makes three Stanley cups in succession, for a new high in the history of the league.

So when the bell rang to end the game Saturday night that gave the Leafs that remarkable record, and the players rushed Turk Broda to laud him by pounding him, embracing him, head-locking him and the Red Wings streamed over to congratulate the man who had clean-swept them for the second year in succession, and the band played, and the announcer on the PA system went to work, and lights played over the ice, who was excited?

Cold as scrooge's heart before he looked in that window? Bland as a croupier raking in the victim's case $50,000? In your hat! Up on my feet braying something into the clamor, pounding the table.

Chills ran down my spine. There was a sensation at the back of my neck as if the hair were standing straight out away from the head and I found time to think it was a good thing I'd had it cut that day or it would have got into the eyes of the people behind me.

And I stood and stood, as did most of the 14,000-odd people there, until there was nothing else to stand for. Then wandered through the Leaf dressing room, or rather wrestled my way around, banging players on the back, even those whom I had reviled at times during the season.

So I'd have to guess the thrill of winning Stanley cups, or world series, or King's Plates, or even quoit championships is here to stay. And a right good thing, too, for the way the brass of the world performs, we can use a few extra moments of pleasure.

All of which is to say "Hurray!" for the greatest hockey machine in the history of the game. Don't get me wrong. I don't mean that this is the greatest team in history. They're far from it. A great team couldn't possibly have given its customers such a poor run for their money during the season. They did what they had to do.

What makes it a great machine is the combination of Conn Smythe and Hap Day, plus their system of feeding players into the machine, their sagacious sorting of material and knitting them into effective combinations.

From practically a standing start, with seven rookies on the club, they bagged the cup two springs back. They were lucky to catch the other clubs crumbling? The Leafs had already crumbled. They came right back for another order last year, and I don't recall where any luck was attached to that.

Now this club lives through a harrowing season, when a natural sag set in because people can't stand prosperity, barely inch into the playoffs and then take it all with the loss

of but one game. Somewhere in there the dynamo that is Smythe, and the cool, wise tireless man that is Day, imbued their charges with the necessary fire.

They were lucky to catch Boston in the semi-finals and then tired Red Wings club in the title bracket? It could have been different? How do we know? We do know that this club got what they needed. They only needed three goals a game to do it. They looked as if they could have got more if necessary.

Now that they've come through a poor season successfully, what's to stop them from making it four maybe five, cups in a row? They can't possibly be as bad next season. The other clubs don't appear to have any bluchers coming to their assistance. The way this machine is travelling, the Stanley cup could be here to stay. And maybe if they win it three or four more years in succession I'll learn to keep cool when the drums go bang and the cymbals clang. ●

NHL President Clarence Campbell presented the 1949 Stanley Cup to Leafs captain Ted Kennedy and his teammates. (Nat Turofsky/HHOF Images)

Bashin' Bill Barilko's Blow Beats Canadiens

Overtime Goal Provides Margin as Leafs Win Another Cup

By Red Burnett • Published: April 23, 1951

Joe Primeau's Leafs, especially one William Barilko, had better preserve the clippings telling of their record-breaking 1951 Stanley cup triumph. Should Willie feel like reminiscing some 20 years hence, he'll need clippings to make the fantastic tale of Saturday's 3–2 triumph over the game but unlucky Montreal Canadiens stick.

It won't be too bad when Willie tells them how he potted the winning goals after 2:53 sudden-death play with the aid of Harry Watson and Howie Meeker. It'll get a little tougher when he tells how every one of the five games played went into overtime, with Leafs winning four of them.

But when he tells them how coach Primeau pulled goalie Al Rollins and how Tod Sloan tied the count with 32 seconds left to play, they're going to demand proof.

The 14,577 who were present at this hockey thriller probably are still pinching themselves to make sure what they saw was true. It's doubtful if any other club ever provided such a sensational climax for a home audience.

This drama-on-ice capped off a series that dripped with thrills, spine chilling moments and reeked with suspense. Every game was in doubt until the sudden-death overtime scores settled the issue.

But L. Standish figured out some doozers for Frank and Dick Merriwell, but never anything to compare with this five overtime games set, which created National Hockey League history and frayed the nerves and vocal cords of capacity puck crowds.

If ever a club received a going over from the fickle finger of fate it was the Canadiens. Battling a superior foe with bulldog courage and tenacity, they needed the breaks to win and got them in only one game, the second, which Rocket Richard won for them.

Saturday, it looked for a time if the Goddess of Luck had switched to their bandwagon. Little Gerry McNeil was performing miraculous feats in their goal and they had beaten our Mr. Rollins twice. The, with just 32 seconds between them and victory, Sloan turned the sweets of victory into the dregs of one of the bitterest defeats in the history of the Stanley Cup.

This was a setting to please the most fastidious director in Hollywood. With just 39

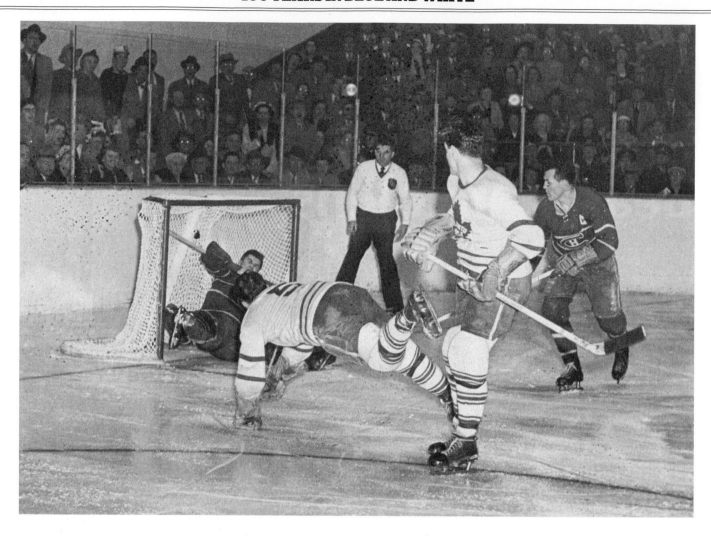

seconds left to play, Primeau flagged Rollins from his goal for the second time after the digging Leafs had forced a faceoff in the Canadien zone.

This was an old story to fans and experts. It was the move used by coaches to give the game that little extra fillip, but one that seldom paid off.

Working the situation to the limit, Primeau took several seconds, it seemed like minutes, to select his six attackers. Out went Kennedy, Smith, Sloan, Thomson, Max Bentley and Watson. Then quickly he sent Mortson out for Thomson.

Joe had tried the same move at 18:33 of the period and was lucky to survive unscathed when Ken Mosdell and his linemates out-wrestled Leafs for possession and almost made it to the unguarded net. Watson saved the situation.

This time, Montreal's Dick Irvin chose Lach, Richard and Olmstead, instead of the Mosdell line, with Boucher and Harvey at the defence posts.

It was a costly switch. Kennedy beat Lach to the draw, got the puck back to Bentley. Max circled out front of the goal and fired skimmer through the maze of arms and legs. Sid Smith raked the puck over to Sloan standing at the crease edge and Sloanie steered it into the open corner.

That took the heart of the Habs, cost them a victory they had locked up. It was like having a man steal home on you in the ninth to tie the score.

Came the overtime and the payoff shot by Barilko, the big defender who opened and closed the playoff sniping for Leafs as they racked up their fourth Stanley cup triumph in five seasons.

Bill Barilko tumbled to the ice as his shot beat Montreal goalie Gerry McNeil in Game 5 overtime to give the Maple Leafs their fifth Stanley Cup in seven years. (Lou Turofsky/HHOF Images)

Pandemonium broke loose in the joint. Primeau hurdled the fence and rushed for Barilko. The players rushed Joe and chaired him.

Howie Meeker, who had been robbed by McNeil on seven previous occasions, started the winning charge. He zoomed into the Canadien zone, failed to click, but followed his shot back of the goal. Beating the defenders to the puck, he passed it out front to Harry Watson who steered it over to one side and Basin Bill steamed up to shovel it home with a slashing backhander. It was as clean as a hound's tooth. McNeil never had a chance.

Pandemonium broke loose in the joint. Primeau hurdled the fence and rushed for Barilko. The players rushed Joe and chaired him. Conn Smythe led Turk Broda on the ice as the fans roared for their favorite fat man.

It was a great night for Barilko and Primeau. For Bill it marked the end of a terrific comeback that started in February. Earlier, he'd been gathering slivers on the end of the Leaf bench, with experts tagging him as a Pittsburgh special. For Primeau it completed a coaching grand slam, gave him Memorial, Allan and Stanley cup triumphs, the first coach to earn such an honor.

It also meant that Joe had filled the largest coaching shoes in hockey, the ones vacated by Happy Day, rated by many as the top coach of all time.

On the night and play, Leafs deserved to win. But for McNeil, they'd have sealed it away in the first period. They outshot Canadiens 41–10 over the 63 minutes and carried most of the play.

However, until Barilko's overtime goal, they were never in front. Rocket Richard, the goal-a-game-demon, sent Canadiens into the lead at 8:56 of the middle period when he took a pass from Bud MacPherson, beat Jim Thomson, the lone defender between him and Rollins, and zipped in to fake Rollins down and out before slipping the biscuit home.

It was 12 minutes even before Sloan took a pass from Ted Kennedy to tie the count. Ted deked Bud MacPherson and Doug Harvey before dumping a pass between them. Sloan had Ed Mazar draped over him like a set shirt when he picked up the puck. But he took the rookie off as he neared McNeil and deked that worthy before flipping home a backhander.

In the third period, the tenacious Habs went in front again when Paul Meger tipped in a shot from Harvey that was deflected to his stock off Joe Klukay's skate.

Then came Sloan's tying counter and the knockout punch delivered by Barilko, who also served both Leaf penalties.

Bobby Dawes and Tom Johnson drew two minute rests and Bill Reay was handed in a 10-minute misconduct for pushing linesman Bill Morrison. Referee Bill Chadwick let a lot go, rather than have penalties influence the tide in this gripping hockey epic.

It was a costly night for Dawes, the ex-Leaf who had spent the previous playoff games on the end of the Canadien bench. Handed the job of checking Ted Kennedy, Bob tried to belt the Left captain into the boards in the second period. He missed and crashed the dasher, suffering a compound fracture of the right leg.

Shortly after the initial face-off, Kennedy fell into the boards and blacked out. He had pinched a nerve near the spinal column and was carried off on a stretcher. However, the pain went as quickly as it had come and Ted was back firing at McNeil two minutes later. A groan went up when he was carried off and he received an ovation when he returned to the wars.

Conn Smythe brought a chuckle from the crowd gathered around the champagne-filled Stanley Cup at the victory party. Lauding Primeau, he chortled: "He's not the guy who's going to retire. It's me" It could be a hint into Leafs' future book. Smythe, who has had more than his share of hockey glory, might be considering moving Hap Day in as team manager. ●

Editor's note: On August 26, 1951, the single engine plane carrying Bill Barilko and his friend, Timmins dentist Dr. Henry Hudson, crashed north of Cochrane, Ontario, killing both men. The wreckage, containing the remains of Barilko and Hudson, was finally discovered in June 1962—just a few weeks after the Leafs won their next Stanley Cup.

Chicago Fans Egg Leafs on to Big Win

Duff Gets Mad at Himself and Scores Cup Winner

By Milt Dunnell • Published: April 23, 1962

Stafford Smythe emerged from self-imposed confinement in a gents' powder room, deep within the Chicago Stadium, and cracked: "You see what happens when they give me absolute authority."

He was kidding, of course. By this time, Punch Imlach had the foot soldiers out of foxholes. They were mauling each other, while Bobby Hull of the beaten Black Hawks organized a make-shift reception line to shake the hands of the new Stanley Cup champions.

In the jam-packed stands, the most partisan, unruly and devoted fans in the world of professional sport—not to mention the most prolific egg-throwers—swallowed their bitter disappointment and applauded, wildly while George Armstrong accepted the length of stovepipe with the howl at the top which is the symbol of world supremacy in hockey.

The stadium organist played "That Old Gang of Mine" and finally, "Auld Lang Syne" as Lord Stanley's silverware was carted away to Maple Leaf Gardens.

The ancient basin probably has been won by greater teams—but it never has gone to a gamer one. Leafs proved last night they're the kind of battlers who swim upstream. At 8:56 of the third period, the dam broke and the flood caught them.

Bobby Hull rapped the puck past Don Simmons for a goal that might have been good enough for all the Easter eggs. Leafs had been the better team, almost from the drop of the puck. They had outshot, out-scuffled and out-hustled the Hawks. None of it had paid off on the scoreboard. Now, the Hawks were in front. With the kind of goal Glenn Hall was playing, there was every chance they would stay in front.

Hull's shot touched off a New Year celebration. Dozens of hats sailed down from the seats. Rubber balls danced like jumping-beans all over the hockey cushion. Red ink stains spread like Toronto blood. It took a good 10 minutes to clear the ice.

Only 93 seconds, by the clock, after disaster struck, the Leafs were back on even terms. In less than six minutes, they were world champions. That was their reaction to adversity. They even gave the script a Hollywood touch.

Dick Duff blamed himself for the Chicago goal. He though he had cleared the puck from back of the Toronto net to Bobby Hull, who eluded a flying tackle by Bobby Baun before making the payoff shot. Hull disagreed with Duff's self-indictment.

Captain George Armstrong posed with the Stanley Cup after the Maple Leafs' victory in 1962. (Lou Turofsky/HHOF Images)

Armstrong probably summed up the feelings of his team when he said: "I've worked all my life to be one of the top 20 pros in this game. That's what I am tonight."

"It was Murray Balfour who gave me the puck", Hull insisted, "so Duff didn't have to get so mad at himself."

Duff was real mad. After Bob Nevin had tied the score, Duff went in with Davey Keon and gave Hall a hard time. At 14:14 while, Eric Nesterenko was serving time for hooking Nevin, the big bomb exploded and Duff was the mad bomber. His able accomplices were George Armstrong and Tim Horton.

"I figured that was the only way I could get even," Duff admitted.

Only 11 years had passed since the night when Joe Primeau, then a first-year coach, added the Stanley Cup to his collection of hockey baubles. Yet, not a single Leaf of that collection was present last night. This was a new generation of Leafs under a new deal in the front office.

Armstrong probably summed up the feelings of his team when he said: "I've worked all my life to be one of the top 20 pros in this game. That's what I am tonight."

Once again, Punch Imlach made a prediction stand up. He vowed to win with Don Simmons in goal—right in Chicago. The Leaf defense rated a big assist in making Punch a true prophet. Many of the Hawks' shots were smothered or deflected before they got to Simmons. When the Redskins did break through, the man in the mask was there to challenge them.

Injured goalie Johnny Bower called it an all-out team effort. And it was that. Leafs shook off the "homer" tag—at a cost to the Gardens of maybe

$40,000. The Stanley Cup comes only once in 11 years. Money comes any time.

Thumbnail tales: Leafs' Tim Horton—probably the most consistently effective Leaf of the entire playoffs—complained that Stan Mikita did a dive which got Horton jugged for a tripping penalty, with only 58 seconds of the game remaining. Questioned on this point, Mikita said he did execute a tumble. But he claimed, Horton had tripped him previously without being penalized....Bert Olmstead, who was on his fifth Stanley Cup club, hinted he might not be back next season. He said this cup winner gave him his biggest lift—because it was the last one.

Red Kelly will take a few days of rest before plunging into the election campaign as a Liberal candidate. Asked if he thought the Leafs' victory would enhance his own chances, Kelly replied:

"Naw, people wouldn't vote for me just because we won the Stanley cup." Well, anyway, it won't keep them from voting for him....Hawks' general manager Tommy Ivan, coach Rudy Pilous, and co-owner Jim Norris all visited the Leaf dressing room to offer their congratulations.

Chicago's tough guy, Reg Fleming, came out of the game with a badly bruised leg. He stopped a hard shot in the first period...The first egg of the game hit the ice as the national anthem ended...Eric Nesterenko, lamenting on the difficulties of covering Frank Mahovlich, sighed: "I let the big sonofagun get away from me." ●

Leafs Are Champions Twice in a Row

Keon Scores Two Goals and Shack Provides the Winner

By Jim Proudfoot, April 19, 1963

Everyone from Mayor Donald Summerville to the Maple Leaf Gardens sweepers jammed into the Leafs' dressing room last night to quaff champagne from the Stanley Cup.

Teetotallers sampled the bubbly on this rarest night of the year, the night Leafs won their second world professional hockey championship in succession, 3–1.

Millionaires, clerks, entertainment stars, fathers, brothers, sons, politicians, hangers-on and scores of newspapermen surged about through wild shouting and glaring flashbulbs in a scene straight out of La Dolce Vita. Players sat around in their steamy underwear or their birthday suits, contemplating the $3,500 jackpot they'd just struck and accepting homage.

The Toronto victory had completed the rout of the Detroit Red Wings and sewed up the title for Leafs, who'd won it in Chicago only 361 days earlier.

Tiny Dave Keon, who scored two of the goals, violated two personal rules. He puffed on a cigarette and downed a few draughts of champagne.

Coughing and sputtering, he explained: "It only happens once a year, you know."

Among those who crowded in to pat him on the back was Mayor Summerville who, it is suspected, would lose to Keon if an election were held today.

Judging by the prolonged ovation he received from more than 14,000 lingering fans last night, Keon is Mr. Toronto for the present.

After Clarence Campbell, president of the National Hockey League, presented the Stanley Cup to Leafs' captain, George Armstrong, in a centre ice ceremony, most of the players withdrew to the dressing room where the celebration was already sizzling. A few veterans remained to participate in television interviews which were carried over the Gardens public address system.

Allan Stanley's speech was drowned out completely as a "we want Keon" chant grew and grew.

Finally, Keon emerged and the old building trembled with applause which abated only while he was delivering a short, shy speech.

"I'm happy we were able to win it here at home and avoid going back to Detroit," he told the mob. Of his goals, he added: "I was lucky."

Earlier, as photographers lined up to get pictures of Armstrong with the Cup, he shouted, "Everybody in here," and gathered all his teammates around him. "It belongs to all of them," he said.

Howe paid tribute to Leafs, saying: "I don't think there's a bad apple in the barrel."

He also spoke of his own club's efforts: "For a team that wasn't even supposed to be in the playoffs, we showed up rather well."

Howe, traditionally unpopular with Toronto fans, was applauded loudly and at length as he skated off. He had played magnificently as he did throughout the play-offs and set up Detroit's one goal scored by Alex Delvecchio.

There were quiet corners in the noisy Leaf room. Bower had a private party, clicking his champagne glass against John Jr.'s ginger ale bottle.

Maple Leaf executives were borne into the showers fully clad and uncomplaining.

Eddie Shack, who deflected Kent Douglas' shot for the actual winning goal, carried the trophy off the ice and into the dressing room. Later, the fans called for Shack, too, but he couldn't make it through the crowd.

Armstrong was the 71st club representative to receive the trophy since Lord Stanley of Preston, Governor-General of Canada, donated it in 1893. This was the ninth victory for the Toronto Maple Leafs and the 12th for a Toronto team.

Much of the credit was given to Johnny Bower, Leafs' 38-year-old goaltender who allowed only 16 goals in the 10 playoff games the victory required.

Bower surprised the Gardens mob with an articulate, typically humble talk in which he pointed out: "It might have gone either way."

The public address system picked up on a comment by Detroit's Gordie Howe: "Thanks to you, it might have gone either way."

Howe was referring to the rousing battle Wings put up right to the finish of last night's match. Bower had to make a dozen fine saves.

Bower went on: "I hope we can win it again next year."

"I'd hold still for this every day," said Harold Ballard, Gardens vice-president, as he disappeared into the deluge.

Also doused were Punch Imlach, the coach and general manager, and president Stafford Smythe.

Imlach found a dry suit to wear to the team party at a midtown restaurant but no spare shoes were available. He was last seen padding up Church St. in his stocking feet.

Carl Brewer was on his way to hospital as his teammates whooped it up. His left arm was broken when he fell heavily into the boards with five minutes left in the game. Earlier it had taken 10 stitches to close a cut inflicted in his mouth by a Detroit stick.

An hour after the game, most of the players had been joined by wives or girlfriends and were on their way to the club party. Outside about 200 young fans waited patiently until the last Leaf was gone.

The players were scheduled to meet in the dressing room this morning to get ready for a ticker tape parade through downtown streets leading to City Hall at noon. ●

Bob Pulford (left) and Frank Mahovlich gave team president Stafford Smythe a good soaking after the Leafs won the 1963 Stanley Cup. (Frank Grant/Toronto Star)

Season Leaves Fans as Exhausted as Leafs

Hurting Team Delivers Third Straight Championship

By Jim Proudfoot • Published: April 27, 1964

It will be remembered as the long season.

The 1963–64 Leafs engaged in 101 games and it's a question who suffered the most, who's the more exhausted today, now that it's all over—Leafs or their harassed, frazzled supporters.

Bobby Baun has his leg in a cast and Red Kelly is in a wheelchair but the team's followers are emotionally spent. An earthquake would make them yawn. The players will be ready for the new season next October but the fans may not make the grade.

Loving the Leafs this winter was synonymous with paranoia. A fan was delirious with joy one day, delirious with worry the next. Leafs had more ups and downs than the stock market. They leaped out of more frying pans into more fires than any club in history.

At the end, after seven months of setbacks and failures, they had their noses in front, like a classy racehorse. Confronted with one climactic match, in which they would win the Stanley Cup or lose it, they produced their finest hockey of the entire campaign and subdued Detroit Red Wings, 1–0.

The season's largest hockey crowd at Maple Leafs Gardens, 14,571, acclaimed Leafs' third successive title with a mighty ovation.

But there were hypocrites in the house.

Folks had been jumping off the Leaf bandwagon since mid-January when they began a 16-game stretch, during which they lost 10 times and scored only 28 goals.

Leafs frittered away the schedule championship they'd been expected to win.

Most of their established heroes were dismayingly unproductive.

The February trade that brought Andy Bathgate and Don McKenney to Toronto, followed by a mild resurgence, was considered an encouraging move.

However, Leafs embarked on the Cup playoffs as a 3-to-1 underdog and proceeded to justify that evaluation by losing three of the first five semi-final matches against Montreal Canadiens.

That was a stern test, even for the most faithful rooter.

Leafs escaped from that predicament, only to find themselves in even more dire straits two weeks later. Wings led them, 3–2 in games, as chapter-six of the final series began last Thursday.

Baun's overtime bouncer won that one and set the stage for Saturday's finale.

On this one vital occasion, Leafs were the hurrying, hurting champions they'd been a year ago and only infrequently this season.

Something new crackled through the Gardens atmosphere right from the start, a sort of collective agreement among the players and their boosters, as if to say: "Okay, enough of this fooling around. Let's get down to business."

The cheering was several decibels louder than usual and Leafs' efficiency was on a higher level, too.

The determination was as tangible in the arena as it had been in Leafs' dressing room before faceoff time.

"I've never seen the team more worked up," said George Armstrong, captain of all three Cup squads.

"There's only one explanation," Armstrong added, "and the best word I can think of is 'heart.'

"Think of what Kelly and Baun went through, playing with those injuries," said Armstrong who himself had received injections to deaden the pain of a damaged shoulder.

"Look at Johnny Bower. How else can you account for him? Hell, he gets tuckered out when we go for a walk in the afternoon. But look at the way he's played.

"And with guys like that coming through, the others have an example to live up to and they dig in and work.

"Listen," Armstrong said, "our jobs were right on the line. We knew that. We had a lousy year, a lot of us. The team did and we're all part of it. If we blew this, we knew darned well there'd be changes next fall. And we knew who'd get the chop—the old guys.

"There was a lot more than the Stanley Cup at stake tonight. It was our jobs and our pride we were fighting for." ●

Nine-year-old Johnny Bower is full of pride as he talks to his father after the game (above). (Frank Lennon/Toronto Star)

MONDAY, APRIL 27, 1964   TORONTO DAILY STAR   PAGE 11

LEAFS IN CUP WINNING RUT--AND EVERYBODY LOVES IT

IT'S THE STANLEY CUP THAT CHEERS FOR MAPLE LEAFS' ALLAN STANLEY AND HIS FATHER
Bill Stanley, Timmins fire chief, has been present at each of Leafs' Three Cup victories

PRIME MINISTER LESTER B. PEARSON HAPPY LEAF FAN
Toronto team hasn't lost at Gardens this season with P.M. there.

Dr. Murray has a fast needle

Four Leaf players punctured

BY JIM PROUDFOOT

Injections of pain-killing drugs kept four Leafs going in Saturday night's Stanley Cup showdown.

Dr. Jim Murray, club physician, said he'd set a personal record for jabbing needles into people.

Two case histories were famous: Bob Baun's broken fibula and Red Kelly's strained knee ligaments. Both were able to skate because Murray's injections numbed the damaged area. Carl Brewer needed injections to ease the discomfort of torn rib cartilage. "I hope I can kick the habit," he said.

And George Armstrong, the team captain, had a damaged shoulder which would have kept him out of the match, if he hadn't been punctured, too. His injury hadn't been made public.

All four played important roles in Leafs' 4-0 victory.

Don McKenney, whose knee ligaments were ripped in an earlier game, was out of hospital in time to see the triumph. It was a doubly memorable day for him; his wife gave birth to a daughter in Boston just a few hours before his first Stanley Cup.

Baun was to have a cast applied to his leg today. Kelly, in agony when freezing wore off, spent Saturday night in hospital but was released yesterday—in a wheelchair. Neither he nor McKenney will require surgery.

Kelly himself hedged but a Liberal party source said that was his last hockey game. Kelly, of course, is the Liberal Member of Parliament for York West.

Tumultuous, dolce vita scenes in Leafs' dressing room are becoming old hat and somewhat forced. Even the cast remains the same.

Champagne flowed Saturday, and so did beer, and there were joyous visitors all the way from Prime Minister Lester Pearson to well-known bookmakers.

It wasn't what you'd call spontaneous. Naturally, the team's owners, John Bassett, Staff Smythe and Harold Ballard, were tossed in the showers.

Other visitors included Mayor Philip Givens, Sid Abel, whose Red Wings were distinguished in defeat, several drunks nobody had ever seen before and some everybody had, and Gordie Howe who toasted Johnny Bower:

"Here's to another six years, you old thief."

Leaf players expressed bewildered pleasure over the weak game Howe had turned in.

* * *

"I'm proud of my team," Abel said. "This was Leafs' best game against us all year and yet it was 1-0 into the third period, and I thought the team that got the next goal would win. We hit a couple of posts. Bower made a big stop on Delvecchio and then Keon got that second goal.

"Leafs are good champions and we're right behind them.

"We were hurt by Doug Barkley's inability to operate normally. His groin injury was okay Thursday but bad tonight."

Keon escaped from Barkley when his goal clinched the Cup.

Abel said there'd be changes in Detroit, adding: "We have some more kids we're high on."

Said Bill Gadsby: "I have to hand it to them—Leafs came up with the big effort. We had our chance to win it Thursday. That's when we blew it."

* * *

Leaf management decides how bonus money will be split. Coming to Leafs are 18 $4,000 cheques. That takes in $500 for finishing third during the schedule, $1,500 for winning the semi-final and $2,000 as Cup champions.

It'll be easy to decide about the regulars, but there were part-time players such as Jim Pappin, Kent Douglas and Larry Hillman and others who came along just for the playoffs.

Wings' bonuses are $2,750 a man.

* * *

Notes: Among Leafs' engagements over the next few days is a trip to Hanlan's Point to plant trees in memory of the late Mayor Don Summerville, who was a devoted Leaf supporter. . . . Carl Brewer leaves almost immediately on an extended European trip, which will include attending university in Paris. . . . Don Simmons, a Stanley Cup man for the third time, said: "To think Leafs had to talk me into coming here." Simmons will teach at a summer hockey school in Bowmanville. . . . Leafs had a hotel party Saturday night, then most of them went to Bob Pulford's place. . . . Wistful onlookers were Dick Duff and Bob Nevin, dealt to Rangers in February. . . . Baun said: "I was assured there was no extra danger in playing with the injury I had."

DETROIT'S GREAT GORDIE HOWE CONGRATULATES THE CHIEF
Defeated Red Wing and Leaf captain George Armstrong in postgame

EASY VICTORY

LIMA, PERU—(Reuters)—The U.S. beat Peru, 59-38, in the women's basketball championships here yesterday.

DAVE KEON ALMOST MAKES IT 5-0 FOR THE LEAFS BUT WING GOALIE KICKED IT OUT
Leaf player swooped in but Terry Sawchuk successfully blocked the scoring try

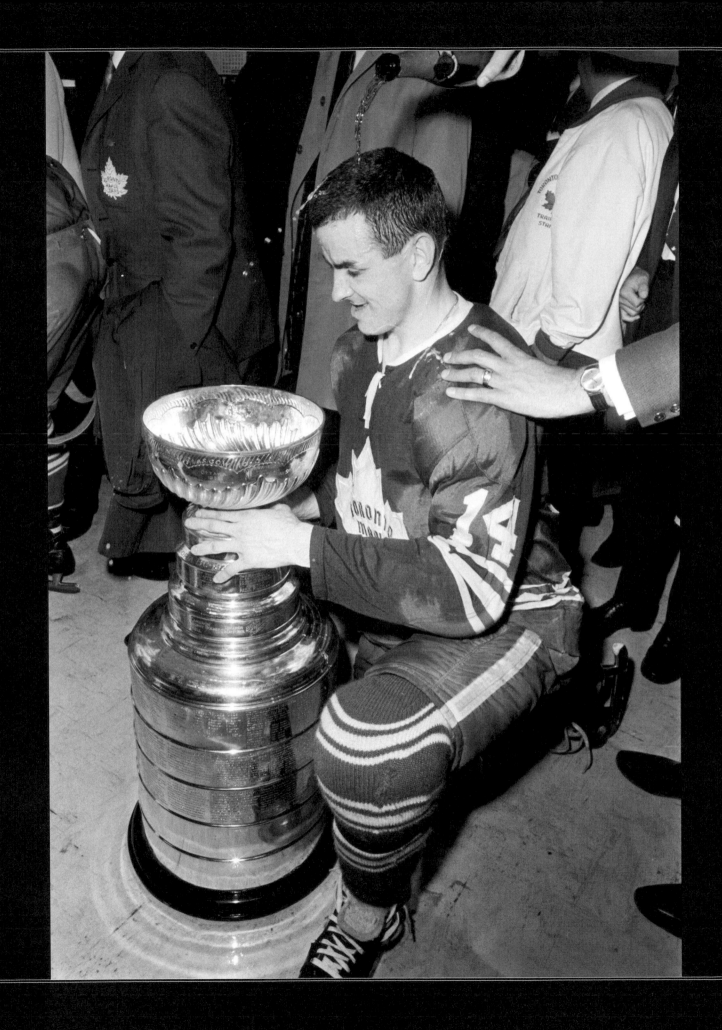

Last Sip from Lord Stanley's Cup

The Leafs charmed run ends abruptly in the first round of the 1965 playoffs and they're eliminated again the following spring but the aging group of hockey warriors rallies for a last hurrah in 1967.

FAST FACTS

- Goaltender Terry Sawchuk, a four-time Vezina Trophy winner, is claimed by the Leafs after Detroit leaves him unprotected in the 1964 NHL intra-league waiver draft.

- Claude Provost's goal at 16:33 of the first overtime period puts a sudden end to the Leafs' playoff run as Montreal wins the semi-final.

- Reginald "Red" Horner, a successful Toronto businessman and onetime badman of the Maple Leafs in the turbulent 1930s, is elected to the Hockey Hall of Fame on June 7, 1965.

- Red Kelly leaves federal politics after serving two terms as the Liberal MP for York West. His successor Robert Winters holds the seat in the November 1965 federal election.

- The goal crease gets a little crowded as netminders Bruce Gamble, Gary Smith and Al Smith are all pressed into service from 1965 to 1967 as Johnny Bower and Terry Sawchuk deal with injuries.

- The Leafs go quietly in the 1966 post-season, managing just six goals as they lose to Montreal in the semi-final in four straight games.

- Jim Pappin begins to skate on a line with centre Pete Stemkowski and wily veteran Bob Pulford. The three players will lead all scorers in the 1967 playoffs, with Pappin bagging the Cup-winning goal in Game 6 of the finals.

- Fan favorite Eddie Shack is sent to Boston for centre Murray Oliver on May 15, 1967 as the post-Cup rebuild begins.

Dave Keon, who led the Leafs in scoring during the 1963-64 season and added 7 goals in the playoffs, took a well-deserved gulp from Lord Stanley's mug. (Frank Lennon/Toronto Star)

Leafs Have Some Housecleaning to Do

Playoff Loss to Canadiens Seals the Doom of Several Players

By Red Burnett • Published: April 14, 1965

Montreal Canadiens' Claude Provost gave Maple Leaf General Manager-Coach Punch Imlach an early start on next season (a rebuilding year) when his backhand loft at the 16:33 mark of overtime ended Toronto's three-year reign as Stanley Cup champion.

That goal gave the speedier, more youthful Habs a 4–3 win and the best-of-seven semi-final, four games to two. It also sealed the doom of a few Leaf veterans and bench-warmers.

While the dashing Canadiens move into the final against the winner of tomorrow night's game between Chicago and Detroit, Imlach will start scouting his rookie prospects at Tulsa, Victoria and Rochester.

Admitting a few had finally played themselves off his team, Imlach snapped: "I hope you noticed my old men weren't on the ice when Provost scored. They nearly won it for me earlier. Gump Worsley robbed Dickie Moore.

"The story of this series was our inability to kill penalties," he added. "there is no question about it.

"Canadiens scored 11 goals on power plays in the six games and we managed only two.

Last year we gave up only two power-play goals in 14 playoff games."

The winners counted three goals in this game while Leafs were a man short and only Provost's came with the sides even Leafs scored twice while playing shorthanded.

But this farewell for several Leafs was a four-star effort. They forced Habs to the limit in a tremendous show that the 14,702 fans who jammed the Gardens will remember for a long time. There wasn't a dull moment in the 76 minutes and 33 seconds of play.

And, once again goalkeepers Worsley and Johnny Bower highlighted the game with spectacular saves. Their work kept the score from hitting double figures as the teams flew with end-to-end rushes.

Canadiens showed tremendous courage and the stamp of true champions when they shook off startling reverses in the form of goals scored against them while they had the advantage and in the loss of star defenceman Jacques Laperriere with a broken left ankle in the third period.

For the first time in the series Leafs came out in high gear and for a time looked as if they'd swamp the invaders.

Johnny Bower made a number of spectacular saves to keep Leafs in the game but Canadiens prevailed in the end. (Frank Lennon/Toronto Star)

"The puck would have hit me in the chest if Kent's stick hadn't deflected it," said Bower. "I just didn't play well enough and Worsley was sensational."

Dave Keon squirted loose from Laperriere, with Leafs two men short and Canadiens one, to put Leafs in front at 2:10.

Red Kelly made it 2–0 with Leafs still short-handed at 3:11. John Ferguson cut the margin with a power-play backhander that just hit inside the cross-bar at 3:32, but Ron Ellis backhanded home Frank Mahovlich's rebound at 3:49 to make it 3–1.

Those four goals, coming in a space of a minute and 29 seconds, set a new playoff record.

Laperriere cut the margin with a screaming slapshot from just inside the blue line at the left point after 9:20 of the second period with Bobby Baun doing time. Bobby Rousseau tied the game on a power play at 6:27 of the third. Provost took the puck away from Ellis to set it up.

It stayed that way until Provost sank the winner.

Bower had no chance, the puck going in off Kent Douglas's stick. Henri Richard lifted the puck out to Provost over a kneeling Tim Horton from behind the Leaf goal.

"The puck would have hit me in the chest if Kent's stick hadn't deflected it," said Bower. "I just didn't play well enough and Worsley was sensational."

Provost said: "Richard's pass was rolling when it came to me but I was all alone and able to backhand it into the net. I was luck."

Whistle-stops: Leafs veterans George Armstrong, Allan Stanley and Ron Stewart all stated they would be back next fall if invited... Dickie Moore and Red Kelly were non-committal and goalie Terry Sawchuk didn't figure he'd be back. "I'll probably be drafted by Boston or some other team," said Terry, but there's a good chance Imlach will protect him in the draft... Referee Jack Ashley handed out 14 penalties, seven to each team... New York coach Red Sullivan picked Claude Provost, Johnny Bower and Bobby Rousseau as the three stars... Ranger goalie Jacques Plante predicted for the television audience that if Canadiens won, it would be on a goal by Provost. ●

The Sentimental Side of Punch

GM Shows Soft Side to Aging Veterans before Big Game

By Milt Dunnell • Published: May 3, 1967

Punch Imlach, the Peerless Leader of the Leafs, is said to have ice water for blood and a paving stone for a heart. In other words, Punch supposedly is as warm and kindly and considerate—according to the charts—as a Moscow cop's handcuffs.

That being the case, he was out of character last night. With all the marbles in the ring, Punch revealed himself as a sentimental creampuff. Before the game, he made a speech in which he said some of his warriors would be playing their last game as members of the club.

"Some of you have been with me for nine years," he went on. It would be nice to say there wasn't a dry eye in the room but it wouldn't be quite right. Several of the serfs fingered their whip scars and waited suspiciously for what would come next.

"It has been said that I stuck with the old men so long we couldn't possibly win the Stanley Cup. For some of you it's a farewell. Go out there and put that puck down their (Canadiens') throats."

Imlach then pointed at a somewhat startled Johnny Bower, the elder statesman of shinny, and told him he was to dress in full regalia and sit on the bench.

Johnny, who confesses to being 42—but never under oath—would have squatted on the time clock in a bikini if Imlach had asked and especially if it would improve his chances of collecting the winners' end of the loot.

But Bower had spent the last five days ducking doctors who sought to punch needles through his leathery hide as treatment for a muscle which popped during the pre-game warm-up last Thursday, night. There was no chance he could go in goal if Terry Sawchuk got hurt.

"You won't be asked to play, but be there," Imlach roared. Al Smith, a third goalie who is too young (21) to be considered seriously by the Leafs for about 15 years yet, was dressed and stashed away in the television room.

Thereupon, one of the elders—a member of the probable departing patriarchs—skated out and robbed the Habs of everything but their underwear. Canadiens are not discouraged easily. Otherwise, Terry Sawchuk would have broken their hearts before the game was 15 minutes old. He did almost as many impossible things as he did in Chicago the day Leafs ambushed the Black Hawks—and as he did in Montreal last Saturday afternoon.

Goalies Terry Sawchuk (left) and Johnny Bower teamed up to lead Leafs to the 1967 Stanley Cup.
(Doug Griffin/Toronto Star)

Thus, the Stanley Cup carnival just ended may become known as the mardi gras of the condemned. Some of the outstanding performers were men who will be marked for exile to the six new expansion clubs--strictly on the basis of age.

This was a Sawchuk who couldn't stop a porcupine with a pike pole last Thursday night.

Frustrated fans had applauded derisively when he cleared a loose puck from the side of the cage. It was the kind of encouragement Dick Stuart, the Old Stonefingers of baseball, used to receive when he picked up a gum wrapper that was blowing across the infield.

"I got mad," Sawchuk admitted last night. "I got mad at myself."

That was when Montreal Canadiens commenced their slide into oblivion, although they didn't realize it at the time. They thought they were lucky in getting rid of Bower, who had allowed only two goals out of 94 shots which the Habs fired at him in two games.

After last night's crushing defeat, the Habs were saying: "First Bower—then Sawchuk. But we might have expected it. They're both old pros. And look at Gump (Worsley) in our net. He hadn't played a full game since March 12. Yet he was great."

Thus, the Stanley Cup carnival just ended may become known as the mardi gras of the condemned. Some of the outstanding performers were men who will be marked for exile to the six new expansion clubs—strictly on the basis of age.

Who was better than Sawchuk—just for openers? He put Leafs into the final round by killing off Chicago. Then he bailed out the good guys, with two key wins after Bower got hurt. He's 37.

Bower is 40-plus. Red Kelly, Allan Stanley, Marcel Pronovost and George Armstrong all are getting extremely long in the tooth. Kelly definitely played his final game as a Leaf. It was his best since the playoffs began.

"There will be something within a day or two," the old redhead promised last night when he was asked about his future plans. It has been practically an accepted thing that Kelly would be named coach at Los Angeles, although no official approach has been made to the Leafs.

Sawchuk denies a story that he would ask to be returned to Detroit. Stanley has no retirement thoughts and no coaching plans. He would like to be back. Sawchuk probably feels the same way. Armstrong, too.

Imlach, though, left them all wondering with his Old Boys' reunion stunt. They probably are wishing he hadn't gone soft and sentimental. Why couldn't he have been his snarly, chilly, impatient, normal self?

THUMBNAIL TALES: When George Armstrong took that pass from Bob Pulford for a goal into the empty Habs net at 19:13 of the third period, he had one thing in mind. "I took careful aim so I wouldn't hit Jacques Laperriere," the Chief said. "I didn't drive the puck, because I wanted to be sure I would hit the net"... Conn Smythe, making his first appearance in the Leaf dressing room in a long time, chortled: "The Smythe name is on the Stanley Cup 11 times now. Who else can say that?"... While champagne was flowing in the Leaf dressing room, Larry Hillman consumed a beer. His explanation: "I'm thirsty."... Dick Duff's goal was a masterpiece. He beat Tim Horton for a shot at Sawchuk, who said: "He deked me, too. I was out of position." ●

Banks will lend $200 million for home building

OTTAWA—(CP-Special)—There's a new $200 million reason why you should find it easier to finance a new home in 1967. Banks are pouring this amount of money or more into house mortgage loans this year, the president of Central Mortgage and Housing Corp. says.

A substantial portion of bank lending will be for urban and surburban housing.

H. W. Hignett said in an interview that the bank loans will boost the number of housing units to be built in the 12-month period, starting June 1, to 170,000.

That number, a "generally accepted" annual construction target, may not be met in this calendar year since the banks have entered the mortgage field only in the last month, he said.

They have been shut out of mortgage lending since 1959 because of legal restrictions on the interest rates they may charge.

But a revision of the Bank Act, passed in late March and effective last Monday, lets the banks into the field at the going mortgage loan rates—7 per cent on NHA-guaranteed loans and around 7¾ per cent on ordinary mortgages.

The huge extra flow of bank money will help loosen the tight squeeze on the supply of lending money for housing.

This squeeze slowed down house building to a walk in 1966.

Metro is expected to be a major gainer from the change.

Bank mortgage loans go as high as 95 per cent of the value of an owner-occupied house worth up to $18,000. The loan percentage generally is 75 per cent of total value for more expensive homes—up to $40,000.

The banks have been preparing for mortgage operations over the last three months, some taking applications in advance of May 1.

Apart from the return to the scene of the eight operating banks, private lenders are also back with the attraction of the higher NHA interest rate.

Life insurance and trust companies had NHA loans for 14,652 housing units approved in the first three months of 1967, more than for the entire 12 months of 1966.

Last week CMHC reported an unprecedented increase in loan applications during March to 23,458 dwelling units.

THE CHEQUE THAT DIDN'T BOUNCE

CANTERBURY (Reuters)—In Britain it is legal to write a cheque on anything.

College student Michael Cain yesterday walked into his bank, put 18-year-old Christina Davidson on the counter and pointed to the writing on her chest above her low-cut dres..

It read, "pay cash five pounds." So bank officials gave him the money (worth $15) and stamped "Paid" on her chest. The money will go to a student-run charity drive.

METRO WEATHER
Thursday sunny with cloudy periods. Warmer. Low 32, high 50. Details page 2.

ESTABLISHED 1892

Toronto Daily Star

four star ★★★★ night

March paid circulation 367,577 copies per day — Wednesday, May 3, 1967—80 pages — 10c per copy, 60c per week home delivery

—Star photo by Bob Olsen

HERO OF LEAFS' Stanley Cup victory, goalie Terry Sawchuk reaches out to rob Montreal of another scoring chance in game Toronto won 3-1, taking cup from Canadiens four games to two. Rushing in to help him are teammates Ron Ellis (8), Allan Stanley (26), Tim Horton (right), Red Kelly (behind). Hab Dave Balon (20) is on the ice and Leon Rochefort (25) turns away.

Tired Terry Sawchuk says 'It has to be the greatest thrill'

By RED BURNETT
Star sports writer

Terry Sawchuk, feature performer in Maple Leafs' 3-1 Stanley Cup triumph over Canadiens at the Gardens last night, seemed to shrink back into his own special corner of the dressing room as boisterous mates whooped it up.

On cloud 9 after dethroning Montreal four games to two in a bruising final, they were swigging champagne and ale and arranging work parties to throw general manager-coach Punch Imlach and his assistant, King Clancy, into the showers.

It was like the CNE midway on Labor Day, but Sawchuk could have been a million miles away as he sipped a soft drink.

"I don't like champagne or ale and I'm too tired to dance around," he said half-apologetically.

Then he rubbed a skinned portion of his face, where a shot had cut right through his mask, and added:

"It may sound corny, but this has to be the greatest thrill of my life. I've had a lot of wonderful moments in hockey and other Stanley Cups, but nothing to equal this.

"First I had that back operation, then Punch had to talk me out of walking out of training camp and quitting hockey.

"Next there was my physical collapse in the Montreal Forum shower in mid-season. I wondered if I'd ever play again. And it wound up in a Stanley Cup win so I guess it was all worth while."

Terry took time out to phone his wife and before ducking out in search of a cool drink, he said:

"It'd be nice to bow out a winner, the first star in a cup-winning game. I have

See GREATEST, page 14

—UPI photo

RID OF HIS MASK, Terry Sawchuk peers into champagne-filled Stanley Cup but settled for a soft drink. He doesn't like champagne.

Shulman charges Wishart condoned 'loaded jury' inquest

Dr. Morton Shulman accused the government yesterday of condoning an inquest which had a loaded jury.

The dismissed Metro chief coroner was testifying at the second day of hearings into his charges that the Ontario government interfered with inquests and suppressed evidence.

Frustrated because he couldn't introduce certain evidence and angry at a series of pointed questions by a royal commission lawyer, Shulman lashed out at Attorney-General Arthur Wishart for "condoning an inquest in which three members of the jury were patients of the doctor involved."

Outside the hearing Shulman said the inquest he was referring to involved the hospital death of Mrs. Pearl Gray in Alliston late in 1964.

At the inquest, held in January in 1965, a coroner's jury found no blame could be attached in Mrs. Gray's death. The jury found she died of kidney failure.

Today, Wishart told The Star: "I have no comment to make until the inquiry is over, unless I am called as a witness. I don't know the case he's referring to. I have no knowledge of it."

Asked if he knew whether he would be appearing as a witness, Wishart said he did not know.

Ontario supervising coroner Dr. H. B. Cotnam today told The Star he could not comment on Dr. Shulman's reference because the commission is sitting.

He said he knew what case Dr. Shulman was referring to and "it doesn't matter to me if it comes up again and is allowed into the hearings; we have a reasonable explantion."

CHIEF ANTAGONISTS

Wishart and Dr. Cotnam have been Shulman's chief antagonists since he was fired for charges he made against the government following a fatal fire March 31 at the Workmen's Compensation Board Hospital in North York.

Yesterday's charge came after a legal wrangle over whether a note from Coroner Dr. Elie Cass to Shulman could be admitted in evidence at the royal commission hearing under Mr. Justice William Parker.

The royal commission was set up by the Ontario government to investigate charges by Shulman that the government had suppressed evidence, interfered with inquests and discriminated against candidates for coroners' posts.

Mr. Justice Parker supported commission counsel Charles Dubin's position that the note should not be admitted at that time.

The exchange followed a statement by Cass that he thought Cotnam would not hesitate to investigate "skulduggery."

Immediately after Shul-

See SHULMAN, page 4

The inquest WAS fair 5 of the jurors insist

Special to The Star

ALLISTON—Three members of a 1965 coroner's jury said today a doctor involved was their family physician and another said he had been treated by the same doctor before the inquest.

A fourth said he had been treated by the doctor prior to the coroner's inquest into the death of Mrs. Pearl Gray, 66, in Toronto St. Michael's Hospital following a hemorrhoid operation in Stevenson Memorial Hospital here.

The four jury members denied that their association with the doctor had "influenced" their verdict—which cleared him of negligence in the woman's death.

One man said the doctor was his family physician before the inquest and still is.

The doctor attended the birth of one of his two children, he said.

TESTIMONY

He said he hadn't given any thought as to why the inquest was held in Alliston and not in Toronto, where the woman died, until reading Dr. Shulman's testimony at yesterday's hearing.

"After thinking about it, it does seem funny that they had it here," he said.

He had not realized he could disqualify himself as a jury member because of his connection with the doctor.

"I think I would have gone ahead anyway. He is treating my family and it would be to my best interests to know," he said.

"My conscience is clear. I came to the only decision I could," he said.

FOREMAN

The foreman of the jury denied that the inquest "involved a loaded jury," as charged by Dr. Shulman.

Dr. Shulman, fired chief Metro coroner, referred to the Alliston inquest yesterday at the inquiry investigating his charges of "cover-up" by Robarts government officials.

The foreman admitted that he was a patient of the physician involved in the operation.

But he denied any conflict of interest. "The inquest was fair and square," he said.

The foreman admitted, as charged by Dr. Shulman,

See THE INQUEST, page 2

Decision at 10:30 a.m.

Court will rule on Truscott tomorrow

OTTAWA (CP-Special)—The Supreme Court of Canada decision on the Steven Truscott case will be given at 10.30 a.m. tomorrow, it was announced today.

The high court has been studying the 1959 murder conviction of Truscott under an order from the federal cabinet.

Three opinions are open to the court. It could recommend a new trial, acquittal or that the conviction be upheld. It will be up to the cabinet to act on the court's opinion.

A spokesman in Prime Minister Pearson's office said today it was likely that any cabinet decision on the Truscott case would be announced in the House which reconvenes on Monday after a week's recess.

The case was referred by the cabinet to Canada's highest court last year, seven years after Truscott, then 14, was convicted in the sex slaying of Lynne Harper, 12, in a wooded area near Clinton, Ont.

Truscott's death sentence was commuted to life imprisonment.

The cabinet decision to ask the high court for an opinion on the case came after Toronto author Isabel LeBourdais wrote The Trial of Steven Truscott, a best-seller which cast doubt on the conviction.

Truscott, now 22, has been held in prison since his conviction. He would be eligible for parole in about two years.

The cabinet referral to the high court asked the justices to consider the existing record, the transcript of the trial, and "such further evidence as the court, in its discretion, may receive and consider."

The review started last October and the court heard a long string of witnesses who had not been present at the first trial.

Truscott himself took the stand for the first time and denied that he killed the Harper girl.

Experts for both the crown and the defence gave conflicting opinions on the question of pin-pointing the time of the girl's death by the contents of her stomach.

The crown used such evidence at the trial to maintain that Lynne Harper was slain less than two hours after she ate her final meal.

The defence called private detectives as witnesses to back up Truscott's story that he was able to see Lynne Harper get into a car on a main highway from a bridge near the Clinton RCAF station where both lived.

Truscott maintained he had given the girl a ride on his bike to the highway and did not see her after she got into the car.

Testimony at the Supreme Court review centred on five points:

1. Was the Harper girl killed between 7:15 and 7.45 p.m. June 9, 1959?
2. Was she killed in the bush near the RCAF station where her partially nude body was found two days later or was the body placed there later?
3. Were sores on Truscott's penis caused by attempted or actual intercourse with the girl?
4. Could Truscott see the girl hitch a ride in the car on the main highway from his position on the side road bridge 1,300 feet away?
5. Was Truscott a normal boy or was he having mental problems?

Toronto Daily Star

Expo's INsecurity

Expo security couldn't handle the crowds that welcomed Haile Selassie—and 59 more state visitors are yet to come, some of them less-loved than the Ethiopian emperor.

Yesterday's attendance of 138,005 brought the fair's total since last Thursday's opening to 1,738,604 — more than twice the 760,400 expected. Page 72.

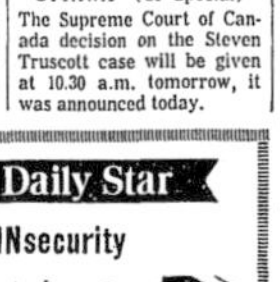

Rich Little hires 2 bodyguards after N.Y. columnist's attack

By LOTTA DEMPSEY
Star staff writer

NEW YORK—Comedian-impressionist Rich Little hired two bodyguards to escort him into the Copacabana night club last night after a columnist accused him of slipping "Soviet sympathy" into his act.

"There are lots of kooks around here and you never know what might happen," said Little's manager, Gib Kerr.

Kerr said an article by Frank Farrell in the World Journal Tribune "accuses Rich of being a Communist."

What upset Farrell was Little's impersonation of President Lyndon Johnson singing a parody of Frank Sinatra's hit, Something Stupid.

Instead of Sinatra's words "and then I go and spoil it all by saying something stupid like I love you," Little has Johnson crooning to Ladybird "and then you go and spoil it all by saying something stupid like Viet Nam."

Farrell calls Little's act "offensive" and snipes: "If Little Rich or Rich Little, or whatever his right British names are, wishes to trample on the American flag or editorialize on our foreign policy, he should do it in Canada."

The part of Farrell's piece that made Little uneasy enough to hire bodyguards at $150 each reads: "The only threat to his (Little's) security will be if he runs into a buddy of those 49 U.S. Marines who were killed in Viet Nam yesterday."

Kerr said it was ironic

See LITTLE, page 9

—Star photo

RICH LITTLE (CENTRE) AND BODYGUARDS
Comedian was accused of "Soviet sympathy" in his act

Quebec Liberals

2 Jewish MPPs called 'racist' by Johnson

By DOMINIQUE CLIFT
Star staff writer

QUEBEC—Premier Daniel Johnson yesterday charged two Jewish members of the Legislative Assembly with practising "racism."

He accused two Liberal members, Victor Goldbloom and Harry Blank, of trying to pin the label of anti-Semetism on the Union Nationale government.

The premier's outburst came after Blank had asked whether the minister of justice would investigate the establishment of a Nazi party in Quebec and look into its proposed training school at Oka, near Montreal

Charges of racism have been flying in the Legislative Assembly ever since former justice minister Claude Wagner was interrupted two weeks ago when Tourism Minister Gabriel Loubier asked "how do you say that in Yiddish?" Wagner is half Jewish.

"The only people who indulge in racism in this House are the two members, Goldbloom and Blank. Theirs is the most subtle and the most efficient way of doing it," Johnson angrily replied yesterday.

Liberal leader Jean Lesage intervened to say that "in the Union Nationale racism and intolerance have been rampant for years."

Johnson shot back: "In due time we will be able to show this province that the real racists are the two members who want to raise this issue, and who are unworthy of sitting in this House to represent the Jewish community if they per-

See QUEBEC, page 8

West may seek Soviet troop deal

LONDON (UPI)—Diplomatic sources said today that the United States and Britain will ask the Soviet Union to cut back its forces in Eastern Europe to match the planned withdrawal of 40,000 allied troops from West Germany

The sources said the Russians may respond favorably, if only because they need the troops to reinforce their defences along the uneasy border with China.

Tired Sawchuk Says 'It Has to Be the Greatest Thrill'

Goaltender Stars as Leafs Beat Habs 3–1 to Win Stanley Cup

By Red Burnett • Published: May 3, 1967

Terry Sawchuk, feature performer in Maple Leafs' 3–1 Stanley Cup triumph over Canadiens at the Gardens last night, seemed to shrink back into his own special corner of the dressing room as boisterous mates whooped it up.

On cloud 9 after dethroning Montreal four games to two in a bruising final, they were swigging champagne and ale and arranging work parties to throw general manager-coach Punch Imlach and his assistant, King Clancy, into the showers.

It was like the CNE midway on a Labor Day, but Sawchuk could have been a million miles away as he sipped a soft drink.

"I don't like champagne or ale and I'm too tired to dance around," he said half-apologetically.

Then he rubbed a skinned portion of his face, where a shot had cut right through his mask, and added: "It may sound corny, but this has to be the greatest thrill of my life. I've had a lot of wonderful moments in hockey and other Stanley Cups, but nothing to equal this.

"First I had that back operation, then Punch had to talk me out of walking out of training camp and quitting hockey.

"Next there was my physical collapse in the Montreal Forum shower in mid-season. I wondered if I'd ever play again. And it wound up in a Stanley Cup win so I guess it was all worthwhile."

Terry took time out to phone his wife and, before ducking out in search of a cool drink, he said: "It'd be nice to bow out a winner, the first star in a cup-winning game. I have a wife, six kids and another on the way. And I miss them very much during the hockey season.

"I'm not saying this was my last game, but I'm going to give it a lot of thought in the next few weeks.

"There's a good chance that I'll call it a day, although I'm not closing the book on hockey at the moment."

Sawchuk treated the 15,977 cash customers and some two million television viewers to one of the finest exhibitions of goaltending in the history of the Cup.

Asked about the long Canadien goal by Dick Duff, the ex-Leaf, Sawchuk said: "He deked me as badly as he deked Tim (Horton). It was a fine move." But the goal proved only that Sawchuk was human.

Goalie Terry Sawchuk was the hero as the Leafs defeated Montreal 3-1 in Game 6 to win the 1967 Stanley Cup.
(Bob Olsen/Toronto Star)

TORONTO DAILY STAR. Wed., May 3, 1967 *15

Leafs capture a Cup ... and here's why

—Star photos by Frank Lennon

TERRY'S TERRIFIC: Leaf goalie Terry Sawchuk was the man most responsible for his team's win last night. Here he stops Dick Duff (6) while Tim Horton (7) pushes aside Yvan Cournoyer and captain George Armstrong (10) watches play.

STOPPED AGAIN: It was a particularly frustrating night for Cournoyer, who is robbed again by Sawchuk as Leafs' Larry Hillman comes to the rescue while Henri Richard of the Canadiens waits in background to see where puck goes.

HE'S GOT IT: Sawchuk drops to his knees to smother a rebound off goalpost with Habs' John Ferguson (22) and—you guessed it—Cournoyer (12) on his doorstep. Leafs are Marcel Pronovost (3) and Allen Stanley. Ref is John Ashley.

"It's almost superhuman the way he's getting in front of some of those Canadien shots," ex-Leaf Joe Primeau had said just before the Montreal goal. "He made a dozen stops that I regard as next to impossible."

Sawchuk made 13 key saves, five in the first period when it looked as if the Habs would stone Leafs and square the series at three wins each, five more in the second and three in the third.

Jean Beliveau, Duff before his goal, Bobby Rousseau, John Ferguson, Ralph Backstrom, Dave Balon and J.C. Tremblay were his chief victims.

With Sawchuk performing miracles in goal, his mates played a dogged positional game, moving in on Gump Worsley when they trapped the Habs or had the edge in manpower.

Red Kelly, playing what is likely his last game as a Leaf, engineered the play that sent his team in front to stay at 6:25 of the second period.

Allan Stanley cleared a pass over the blue line and Kelly caught up with it just over the red line. He deked two defenders to blast a shot off Worsley and Ron Ellis dashed in to pot the rebound.

The winner by Jim Pappin was tainted, as is often the case with big Stanley Cup goals. He tried to feed Pete Stemkowski a backhand pass in the goal-mouth and the puck caromed in off Jacques Laperriere, who had Stemmer locked up.

Just when it looked as if there was no way the Habs could pierce the armor of a sensational Sawchuk, Duff scooted around Horton and zipped a backhander home at 5:28 of the last period.

From then until captain George Armstrong pounded a long shot into the Canadien goal with 47 seconds left, it was a tense, gripping duel between a desperate offence and a stubborn, clever defence.

Coach Toe Blake lifted Worsley at 19:05 for an extra attacker after Leafs were called for icing.

Allan Stanley beat Beliveau to the faceoff and cleared him out of the way with his body to allow Kelly to relay the puck to Bob Pulford, who fed Army in the clear. ●

Captain George Armstrong and Harold Ballard with the Stanley Cup (left) at city hall in Toronto after the Leafs' victory in 1967. (Dick Darrell/Toronto Star) Banner (right) celebrating the Leafs' last Cup win hangs from the rafters at the Air Canada Centre. (David Cooper/Toronto Star)

'It Was Our Last Kick at the Bucket'

By Paul Hunter and Joseph Hall • Published: April 7, 2012

The day's mail almost always includes a few items for Red Kelly to autograph and return. It's part of the 84-year-old's routine. But a photo arrived at his Toronto home a few days ago that caused him to pause. It was a picture of the Leafs '67 Stanley Cup winner.

"I was just looking at the picture of that team and thinking, 'Holy man, we won the Cup?'" he says, incredulity in his voice.

"We really were the over-the-hill gang and we made it. Looking at the team, you'd say, 'Boy, there had to be a lot of good things happen there.' I was thinking (coach Punch) Imlach must have done a pretty good job. I know a lot of people were mad at him, a lot of players were upset with him, but he was smart behind the bench, putting the right players out in a game."

One of the good things, of course, was Kelly. He'd been a Norris Trophy winner as the league's top defenceman with Detroit, where he won four Stanley Cups before moving on to Toronto. He won another four championships after the Leafs converted him to centre.

But as much as he admired Imlach's strategizing, Kelly recalls that an illness that knocked the autocratic coach out of commission for 10 games helped turn around the club's fortunes that season.

Toronto had struggled through a 10-game losing streak that dragged into early February. When Imlach was rushed to hospital with what were believed to be heart problems in mid-February, upbeat team executive King Clancy took over behind the bench and his easygoing approach was a tonic for the stressed team.

Clancy kept everyone energized, curtailed the grueling workouts and, essentially, rolled his lines. Kelly recalled that the unit of Bob Pulford, Pete Stemkowski and Jim Pappin—put together by Clancy—got hot and continued their torrid scoring once Imlach returned late in the season. The production from young players such as Stemkowski and Pappin would prove crucial to the Stanley Cup win. Clancy stepped aside with a 7–1–2 record as interim coach.

Even as Kelly was edging toward his eighth Stanley Cup, he knew the end of his career was at hand. He'd also served for three years as a Liberal member of Parliament during his Leafs run and was becoming increasingly fatigued with the toll that simultaneous careers in politics and hockey were taking.

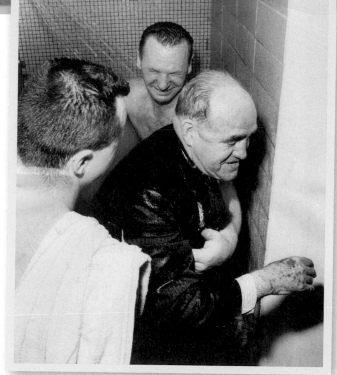

However, he was playing so well—he picked up two assists in the Cup-clinching game—that the Leafs offered him a four-year contract extension. Driving to Maple Leaf Gardens on the day of Game 6, Kelly told his wife Andra that it was going to be his last game if they won.

"I was just, 'You can't let down.' We had to fight right till the end. Now we can let down. You were happy but it was the end now."

Andra says she didn't see much of that last game because she had tears in her eyes.

"I knew it was the end of a wonderful time," she says. ●

Members of the Leafs' 1967 Cup-winning team were honoured (top) before a game in 2007. (David Cooper/Toronto Star) At right, King Clancy celebrated with Johnny Bower after the 1967 win. (Frank Lennon/Toronto Star)

The Wilderness Years

The 22 seasons following the 1967 Cup win are a combination of ineptitude and unfulfilled promise. Other than a semi-finals win over the Islanders in 1978, The Leafs finish out of the playoffs in seven of those seasons and don't advance beyond the second round in 15 others.

FAST FACTS

- The teardown/rebuild of the Cup champion Leafs proceeds in earnest on March 3, 1968 when Frank Mahovlich, Gary Unger, Pete Stemkowski and the rights to retired defenceman Carl Brewer are traded to Detroit for Norm Ullman, Paul Henderson, Floyd Smith and Doug Barrie.

- Dave Keon takes over as Leafs captain, succeeding George Armstrong, at the start of the 1969-70 season.

- Hall of Fame goaltender Terry Sawchuk, aged 40, dies after wrestling with former Maple Leafs teammate Ron Stewart in May 1970. The death is ruled accidental.

- Punch Imlach, who has guided the team to four Stanley Cup titles, is fired after the Leafs miss the playoffs in 1969.

- A series of coaches try, but ultimately fail, to match Imlach's success: John McLellan (1970), Red Kelly (1974), Roger Neilson (1978), Floyd Smith and Dick Duff (1980), Joe Crozier and Mike Nykoluk (1981), Dan Maloney (1985), John Brophy (1987) and George Armstrong (1989).

- Leafs continue their rebuild with key draft picks of Brad Selwood (1968), Darryl Sittler and Errol Thompson (1970), Pat Boutette (1972), Ian Turnbull and Lanny McDonald (1973) and Dave "Tiger" Williams and goaltender Mike Palmateer (1974).

- Stafford Smythe, the principal owner of the Leafs since 1961, dies of a bleeding ulcer on Oct. 13, 1971, aged 50. He is succeeded by Harold Ballard.

- Darryl Sittler sets an NHL record on Feb. 7, 1976 by scoring six goals and adding four assists as the Leafs slam Boston 11-4. The 10 points is a record that still stands—no other player has had more than eight points in a single game.

- Another rebuild begins in 1980 with the acquisition of Rick Vaive via trade and the draft additions of Bob McGill (1980), Jim Benning (1981), Gary Nylund, Gary Leeman, Peter Ihnacek and Ken Wregget (1982), Russ Courtnall (1983), Al Iafrate and Todd Gill (1984), Wendel Clark (1985), Vincent Damphousse (1986) and Luke Richardson (1987).

- Darryl Sittler is traded to Philadelphia in January 1982 for Rich Costello, a second round draft pick and future considerations.

- Rick Vaive scores four goals on March 22, 1982 in the Leafs' 8-5 victory over Chicago, giving him 49 for the season and breaking the team record of 48 goals, set by Frank Mahovlich in 1961.

- Forwards Rick Vaive and Steve Thomas and defenceman Bob McGill are traded to Chicago for Ed Olczyk and Al Secord in September 1987

- Punch Imlach and his close sidekick King Clancy die a year apart—Clancy first in November 1986, aged 83, and Imlach in December 1987, aged 69.

Leafs captain Darryl Sittler's 10-point effort vs. Boston in February 1976 still stands as an NHL record.
(Ron Bull/Toronto Star)

Salming a Solid Factor in Rebirth of Leafs

Rookie Defenceman Blends Aggressiveness with Superb Skills

By Frank Orr • Published: February 9, 1974

The weekly publicity release which accompanies the National Hockey League scoring statistics clattered off the teletype in Maple Leafs' executive suite this week.

Immediately, a telephone call was made to NHL headquarters in Montreal to inquire if the chaps who beat the drums for the league had taken leave of their senses.

The release listed the top rookies in the NHL this season, and Borje Salming's name was omitted. Around Maple Leaf Gardens this season, such an oversight is dangerous for the men who make it.

"We were a little upset about Salming's name not being included," said Leaf general manager Jim Gregory. "We feel he rates with the best rookies in the league. The NHL release was based on scoring statistics and Salming didn't have enough points to qualify. But there is much more to evaluating a player than his point total."

No doubt about it: Salming is one-two with anyone as the NHL's best freshman. In fact, he's one of the best defencemen, period.

In partnership with another precocious fresh, Ian Turnbull, Salming is a big reason for Leafs' return to NHL respectability. Upgrading of the club's defensive performance is a major factor in the rebirth. Although good goaltending has assumed a big role, too, the work of the green back-liners is pivotal.

Salming's scoring statistics, one goal and 21 assists, are representative of his total effort for Leafs this season—solid rather than spectacular. In the more-revealing "plus-minus" numerals, Salming has a plus-30, the best Leaf mark.

The plus indicates the difference between goals for and against his team when a player is on the ice in equal manpower situations. While no statistic is all-conclusive, Salming's high plus indicates he's a very positive factor, both in production and prevention of goals.

Of the rookies, only Al Sims of Boston Bruins had a higher plus at the halfway point of the season. But Sims' total was accomplished as Bobby Orr's blueline partner and it's sagged during Orr's absence with a knee injury.

Salming faces a tough battle to earn the recognition he deserves in the Calder Trophy ballot boxes. Atlanta Flames' publicity department will flack outrageously for centre Tom

Defenceman Borje Salming was the complete package of offensive and defensive skills. (Jeff Goode/Toronto Star)

Lysiak, New York Islanders' for Denis Potvin and Bob Nystrom, and St. Louis Blues on behalf of John Davidson.

Leafs, and most establishment teams, never have indulged in such tub-thumping for their trophy candidates. Leafs have an additional problem in lobbying for Salming. He's one of their five good rookies (Turnbull, Inge Hammarstrom, Bob Neely and Lanny McDonald are the others) and management feels that a publicity campaign for one hardly would be fair to the others.

It might not be necessary because Salming slowly has impressed everyone around the NHL. When Leafs brought Salming and winger Hammarstrom from Sweden, they faced the NHL view that Swedish hockey players weren't very brave and NHL-style intimidation would send them packing back to the effete hockey of their homeland.

The "chicken Swede" segment of Salming's big league baptism is almost over. Now he and Hammarstrom can play their game with no special designations of race (Swedish) or colour (some foes figured it was yellow).

"I haven't heard 'chicken Swede' for quite a time," Salming said. "That happened a few times early in the season, which seems ages ago now."

Occasionally, an opposition bully gives him a cheap shot but Salming is chicken in the same way that Lena Horne is homely and J. Paul Getty is poor.

Salming doesn't bop people on the head with his stick or crash them into the boards or pick fights, all those lovely traits which a man must possess to be qualified as brave by the NHL hair-shirts. He does get in attackers' way and tangles them up in front of the net and drives fearlessly in front of shots.

Salming has abundant aggressiveness and muscle, attributes which he's blended with his skills. In his style, removing the puck from an attacker's possession with deft poke-check produces the same result as knocking him on his drawers. A sweep check has the same affect as a slash.

Not that Salming can't throw body-checks or apply his tick to opponents. He does that when situation demands it. But he docsn't need those things to be effective.

Salming is not especially flashy. He's 6 feet tall but his long legs make him appear very lanky. Although he skates with what seems a laboring stride, his speed is surprising when rated in a race with an established fleet mover.

In fact, Salming is deceiving in many areas. He weighs 200 pounds but looks frail, and he has surprising strength from a body that is all elongated muscle.

His reach caused one wit to compare him to "Plastic Man," the old comic book hero whose arms and legs could stretch for miles. Foes figure they've eluded Salming only to have the puck hooked away from what seems an impossible distance.

Salming's brilliance, plus Hammarstrom's 15 goals, makes Leafs' Swedish venture a rare coup. The $100,000 which Leafs paid the Swedish hockey body for their releases was an immense bargain.

For Salming, the decision to migrate to the NHL created the need for a big adjustment in his lifestyle. But it also fulfilled a long-time ambition to make hockey his profession.

"I'd played hockey from the time I was 7 years old and practiced very hard at the game," Salming said. "I tried to be a good student but all I wanted to do was play hockey. I wasn't very good in school because most of the time, I was too tired from playing hockey.

"To become a professional in Sweden was impossible. I played for Brynas team in the top league and was on the national team, but I had to have a job as a machinist to make a living. Coming to the Maple Leafs gave me a chance to do what I like best and earn good money. That's why I moved to Canada.

"Some people in Sweden told me that I'd go to the NHL and come back a cripple. Others said Inge and I were doing a bad thing for our country by leaving the national team. But most people were behind us because

Forwards Darryl Sittler (left) and Lanny McDonald and defenceman Borje Salming formed the nucleus of the Maple Leafs in the 1970s. (Frank Lennon/Toronto Star)

"In his mind, he's never beaten by a forward and he never quits. He's a very smart player in addition to all his skills."

in Sweden, they follow the NHL closely and know it's the best league in the world."

Salming understood English better than he spoke it, at first, but he's greatly improved his conversation powers. His close friend Hammarstrom and his girl-friend Margitta handle English fluently.

The Leaf players, who gave him the nickname B.J., helped in the adjustment to Canadian life, and Salming looked after the hockey switch himself.

"The players have been just great to Inge, Margitta and me," Salming said. "The team is like a big family. They invite us to their homes and do everything they can to make us welcome. Because of this, we haven't been homesick once.

"Sure, they've made many jokes at us but we make a few at them, too. When the team was on a long road trip last month, Margitta was skiing or shopping with the players' wives just about every day."

In European hockey, Salming was an offensive defenceman, but he's modified that approach. His part-ner Turnbull is the prominent rusher.

"When I saw that Ian was such a good rusher, I played more of a defensive game," Salming said. "I've been carrying the puck more lately."

Salming had assorted adjustments to make from the style of hockey players on the wider European rinks to the more physical, close-quarters combat of the NHL.

"I had longer blades on my skates in Sweden because we didn't play so much close to the boards," Salming said. "I had to shorten them a couple of inches here because a defenceman in the NHL must work a great deal in the corners.

"Everything happens much more quickly in the NHL, especially in the corners. There isn't as much time to do things before a checker is on top of you. I had to learn to make things happen more quickly.

"When the Swedish national team played Team Canada in 1972, we saw how good the NHL players were. We knew that it would be difficult to play in the NHL and it's even better than we thought. That's why I was very happy to make the team and play as much as I have. Both Inge and I are much, much better hockey players than we were in September."

Leaf vice-president King Clancy calls Salming "the best defensive defenceman in the NHL." Gerry MacNamara, who scouted Salming for Leafs in Sweden, claims the Swede's absence from the all-star team "indicates that there must be one great crop of defence-men in the NHL."

"The reason Salming is so good is because he gives so much effort," said Marlboro coach George Armstrong. "In his mind, he's never beaten by a for-ward and he never quits. He's a very smart player in addition to all his skills." ●

Leafs vice-president King Clancy called Borje Salming "the best defenceman in the NHL." (Dick Darrell/Toronto Star)

NHL Bullies Are Tiger's Cup of Tea

Williams Doesn't Know the Meaning of Fear

By Rex MacLeod • Published: February 22, 1978

There is one constant when the Toronto Maple Leafs play—Tiger Williams is about to get a penalty or has just been paroled.

The Tiger is closing in on 300 penalty minutes for the season. he had 338 minutes last year but he humiliated himself the year before with a mere 299.

Mention Tiger Williams and hockey fans get a mental image of penalty boxes, gloves on the ice and disheveled grapplers.

Actually Williams, give or take a few head butts, is—in the opinion of his peers and coaches—a solid, systematic hockey player. If he were available he would be snapped up but Leafs, no matter how hard they try, cannot dispose of more saintly types.

Most coaches admire Tiger's pugnacity. He doesn't know the meaning of fear, one of the few four-letter words that stump him. He will take on an entire team, collectively or individually, and give them the choice. He contends he has never lost a fight. If you want to quibble about his points system, take it up with him.

He has 16 goals for the season and his coach, Roger Neilson, winces every time he gets another one. The Tiger does such a contorted roundelay when he scores there is acute danger he could ruin himself. The survivor of a thousand fights could cripple himself in a victory twist.

Neilson, a cerebral coach, warmly endorses the Tiger. So do most of his teammates. Of course, if they don't, the Tiger might beat the hell out of them.

"He's very alert," Neilson said. "He notices things—like line changes. He's the first guy out. Skating? I don't know what it was like before, but his skating is all right. He can't do everything he wants to, but he's okay."

Tiger says he had a team meeting with himself at a young age and deduced that if he couldn't skate he should acquire other talents if he wanted to succeed as a pro hockey players. Actually, he is not the worst skater on the Leaf team, but that isn't a glowing recommendation.

"I figured a guy who can't skate must have two other things going for him," he says. "Number one, he must have stronger legs than most and number two, he must be in better condition. I've worked on those things.

"Another thing that helped me was that Red Kelly (Leafs' ex-coach) told me I should never, at any time, skate less than three-quarters all out. I figured Red, one of the greatest skaters in the game, knew what he was talking about. In all the drills I concentrate on those points."

Tiger Williams was willing to take on a whole team, collectively or individually. (Toronto Star)

"The thing to remember is if you're gonna fight, you gotta win. If not you don't help your team or yourself. Right now I'm winning, so why change?"

Tiger concedes his skating has improved since he joined Leafs in 1974, but he suspects it might be overemphasized by analysts trying to figure him out. Any improvement, he says, is due mostly to maturing.

"Very few guys come into this league and click right off the bat. (Mike) Bossy? Wait till the playoffs. If I was checking him he wouldn't get a goal, unless it was on a power play."

Some notorious NHL toughies in the past made their reputations by beating up smaller opponents. The Tiger, at one time or another, has challenged all the bare-knuckle or knuckle-head club heavyweights. Doesn't he get scared once in a while?

"I'm not worried about anybody," he says—no chest pounding, no histrionics. There are no phony dramatics with the Tiger. Whatever he is, he's authentic.

"It's part of my living," he continues. "I've got a job in the NHL and I'm very good at it. In four years in the league I fell on my ass only once in a fight—with Guy Lapointe and he's a nice guy. He doesn't even fight. I stepped on a stick and wound up on the bottom. That's the only time."

Tiger philosophizes that there is no point in fighting merely for fighting's sake. You can get hurt that way.

"The thing to remember is if you're gonna fight, you gotta win. If not you don't help your team or yourself. Right now I'm winning, so why change?"

There is a theory that some NHL players—say with limited talent and an abundance of ambition—feel fighting is necessary to get established. Once established they become law-abiding, hockey-playing citizens. Does Tiger, for instance, still need to keep proving himself?

"More than ever," he replies. "The league is stronger now than when I broke in. Guys have come back from the WHA. Fighting used to be something to do for a guy because he only got on the ice once in a while and he might have to use that chance to get noticed. That isn't necessary anymore."

Some of the NHL's more active pugilists in the past gradually reformed because—apart from split lips and splintered teeth—they found fighting on ice immensely tiring.

"It's tiring for guys who don't, as a rule, fight," Tiger concedes. "They have a fight and they're finished for the entire period. Me, I'm used to it. You gotta be good at it. Sure, I'm tired after the skirmish but five minutes in Millhaven and I'm ready to go again."

But, like the gunslinger in the old west, he sees no peace ahead, no chance to settle down. He won't be allowed to hang up his fists even if he feels that way. It is unlikely he will ever be in the running for a Lady Byng award.

"It won't come to that point," he says. "Humans will always be frustrated and must take it out on someone." ●

Coach Roger Neilson winced every time Tiger Williams went into his goal-scoring celebration. (Doug Griffin/Toronto Star)

Leafs Off to Montreal Thanks to McDonald

Overtime Goal Ends Bitter Series Against Favoured Islanders

By Frank Orr • Published: April 30, 1978

Lanny McDonald's booming shot, which had won assorted games for Maple Leafs during the past three seasons, couldn't get the job done but his soft one did.

Hampered by an injured wrist, McDonald lofted a shot over the glove of New York Islander goalie Chico Resch at 4.13 of overtime to give Maple Leafs a 2–1 victory in the seventh game of the Stanley Cup quarter-final series last night in Uniondale, N.Y.

Leafs' surprise elimination of Islanders sends them into the semi-finals for the first time since 1967. They'll meet the powerhouse Montreal Canadiens in a best-of-seven series opening Tuesday evening in Montreal.

After Leaf goalie Mike Palmateer, superb throughout the series, had stopped Islanders Bill Harris on an in-alone chance, another brilliant playoff Leaf, defenceman Ian Turnbull, choreographed the winning goal.

"It's a play we've tried a few times in practice but we needed a little luck to make it work," McDonald said.

"Turnbull brought the puck up the ice and I cut into the middle to spread the defence. He flipped a high pass to me which hit an Islander (Stefan Persson), hit me and dropped at my feet.

"All of a sudden, there was nobody between me and Resch and I needed an instant to realize that I was in the clear. Chico came out to cut down the angle and I had to get the puck over his glove, I did."

McDonald, considered removing his face mask after regulation time.

"A couple of times I lost sight of the puck because of the mask," said McDonald, who was wearing the protection because of a broken nose.

"Yeah, he wanted me to take it off," said trainer Guy Kinnear afterwards. "I told him if he was hit again that would be it for the season."

"Guy didn't want me to take it off but said I'd score the winning goal anyway," said McDonald.

The goal ended one of the National Hockey League's best—and most bitter—playoff series in recent years. Leafs said from the outset that their plan was to out-hit Islanders—and they did.

Their play brought charges of vicious, chippy work from the Islanders and an avalanche of criticism of Leafs' grinding approach. Although their physical aggression made some Islanders play tentatively, the Toronto club's disciplined checking, which granted the New

Lanny McDonald put the finishing touches on his stick before scoring the winning goal in overtime as the Leafs upset the Islanders. (Keith Beaty/Toronto Star)

"Hitting is the basis of good defensive play and our guys, to a man, were committed to it."

Yorkers little room to operate their smooth attack, was the key factor.

That—and the brilliance of Palmateer—gave Leafs a large upset.

"No matter what anyone says, we weren't trying to intimidate the Islanders," said Leaf coach Roger Neilson. "We had to play physical hockey to have a chance against a really fine team with a great deal of offensive sting.

"Hitting is the basis of good defensive play and our guys, to a man, were committed to it. We had a big effort from every guy on the team but we had some great individual performances.

"Palmateer had a very big part in the win. Any time a goalie holds Islanders to 13 goals in seven games, he's playing superbly. Turnbull was just outstanding in every game."

Leafs' chances to win the series took a serious nosedive when their all-star defenceman Borje Salming sustained an eye injury in the fourth game and missed the duration of the series. However, Randy Carlyle, who hadn't played in a month, stepped in and did an excellent job.

Denis Potvin gave Islanders a first period lead and Turnbull, who once was Potvin's defence partner with Ottawa in junior hockey, tied it for Leafs in the second period.

The goaltending of the two little men, Resch and Palmateer, was again the highlight of the match.

Leafs opened the game with their promised aggressive play but abandoned that approach as the game settled into tight-checking hockey. Islanders carried the attack into the Leaf zone in the early going which reduced the Leaf opportunities to hit.

A Leaf mix-up in their own zone created the opportunity for Islanders' opening score. A Leaf clearing attempt bounced into the middle of the ice, directly into the possession of Potvin. He skated up the slot and beat Palmateer with a 20-foot wrist shot .

While Leafs had few good scoring chances against Resch in the first period, Islanders made life hectic for Palmateer. He made a big pad save on Bob Nystrom on a good move by Bob Bourne down the wing, then stopped Billy Harris on an in-alone chance.

In between those chances, Islander defenceman Dave Lewis bounced a shot off the goal post from the blueline.

The period ended with Islanders on a power-play and defenceman Persson protesting to referee Andy Van Hellemond. Persson had been attempting to hold the puck inside the Leaf zone along the boards in front of the Toronto team's bench when he suddenly fell to the ice. Persson claimed that a Leaf on the bench had pushed him.

A desperation dive by Palmateer prevented Islanders from building a two-goal lead early in the second period. He was caught far out of the net and Islanders' Bryan Trottier had the open net into which to slide the puck. However, Palmateer sprawled with this stick extended to block the shot.

Jimmy Jones and Pat Boutette did the spadework on the tying goal. Boutette carried the puck deep into the Islander corner, then Jones took over and moved behind the net.

Although harassed by a defender, Jones managed to one-hand a pass into the slot from where Turnbull blasted home his fourth goal of the playoffs.

Although the Leafs did play strongly through the middle minutes of the period, it was Islanders again who had the big chance. Jones lost the puck in the Leaf zone granting Mike Kaszycki a clear chance. But the Islander centre's pass hit the crossbar.

The only serious skirmish of the period saw Leafs' Trevor Johansen and Garry Howatt of Islanders stage a brief fight.

Leafs held an 11–6 edge in shots on goal in the period and one tally had them on top in hits, too, by a 17–3 margin. ●

Storm Hits Leafs Locker Room

Players in State of Near-Shock after MacDonald Traded

By Jim Kernaghan • Published: December 29, 1979

Within a couple of shattering moments yesterday, the turbulent world of the Toronto Maple Leaf hockey club exploded into its stormiest phase of a decidedly tempestuous season.

Leaf general manager Punch Imlach walked quietly into the office of coach Floyd Smith and asked the coach to send in Lanny McDonald and Joel Quenneville, shortly after the team had come off the ice from practice at Maple Leaf Gardens.

In the office, adjoining the team dressing room, Imlach informed mainstay right winger McDonald and promising young defenceman Quenneville they had been traded.

Moments later, there was a deafening slam of the door and McDonald, fiery-eyed, stomped out of the Gardens.

According to someone with access to what went on in the office "Imlach started out by telling Lanny, 'This is the hardest part of my job...'"

He didn't get to finish. McDonald demanded to know to whom he'd been traded and for what. Imlach informed him that he was going to Colorado Rockies but that the announcement would not be official for a couple of hours and he could call back.

McDonald's response is unprintable.

As it evolved, McDonald and Quenneville go to Denver for left winger Pat Hickey and right winger Wilf Paiement. Hickey is to arrive in Toronto this afternoon and play tonight but Paiement, whose wife is expecting a child any moment, did not indicate when he'd arrive.

Quenneville is expected to play for Rockies tonight in Denver but it is uncertain whether McDonald will get there for that game.

The reaction in the Toronto dressing room was immediate. Players filed out in a state of near-shock, Quenneville among them.

"I can't believe it's happened," Quenneville said, "What can I say? Mackie and I are gone."

Other players had plenty to say. Tiger Williams strode immediately to a telephone and called his lawyer in Calgary, Herb Pinder. Others predicted the destruction of the Maple Leaf team was approaching completion.

Still in the dressing room, Floyd Smith, clearly unaware as to what would happen when Imlach summoned the players, paced the floor, ashen-faced.

"Are they trying to destroy this team?" asked one irate Leaf.

Others claimed to be looking for ways out, that they never would play for Imlach again. Others simply shook their heads.

Inside the dressing room, alone, sat captain Darryl Sittler, McDonald's closest friend and half of the one-two punch they have constituted over the years. Tears welled in his eyes. He could not speak.

"I've been getting traded for the last four years, it seems," said defenceman Ian Turnbull, long a subject in trade rumors.

"Mackie is the top all-around right winger in the league," commented another defenceman, Dave Hutchison.

"Joel was the best defenceman on the ice against Buffalo Sabres," added Walt McKechnie of Leafs' last game.

Inside the dressing room, alone, sat captain Darryl Sittler, McDonald's closest friend and half of the one-two punch they have constituted over the years. Tears welled in his eyes. He could not speak.

There was dismay and anger among those who did not speak, some of whom saw this trade as the final stroke of a season-long campaign to break Sittler.

"Imlach had to get rid of one of them to show his strength," said one, who shall remain anonymous. "He couldn't get rid of Darryl because of that clause in his contract (Leafs must pay Sittler $500,000 if they trade him) so they got at him another way by trading Lanny."

Another Leaf said the hand-writing was on the wall the day Imlach took charge last summer.

"What he said, in effect, was that this team had five good players and the rest were no good," he said. "Great way to start, eh? I thought at the time, my God, this franchise could crumble with that outlook.

"Well, it seems to be now. And some of you guys (reporters) are partly to blame for getting (Jim) Gregory and (Roger) Neilson fired by so much criticism of the defensive philosophy they had.

"Now, with all the crap that has been laid on us by Imlach, it's difficult to even concentrate in a game nowadays. The pressures have been unbelievable. And the worst part is, they're needless."

Imlach issued a statement to the effect that trading players is always a difficult thing to do but must be done for the betterment of the club.

Ray Miron, Colorado general manger, expected Quenneville early today and hoped that McDonald could make it for Rockies' game tonight, a sell-out match against Philadelphia Flyers.

"We see Quenneville as a player of great potential and we know what Lanny can do," Miron said. "It was a deal that was just consummated. We've only been talking a few days. I see it as a good trade both ways.

"We sure hated to give up a guy like Paiement, one of our original players. But he wasn't producing. After we got Pat from the Rangers, he started really well but hasn't been consistent. Between them, they have the ability to score 60 to 70 goals."

Hickey has eight goals and 10 assists and Paiement, 10 goals, 14 assists. McDonald has produced 15 goals and 15 assists for Leafs this season and Quenneville had a goal and four assists.

On balance, the trade seems equitable. Financially, Toronto takes on a slightly heavier load. Paiement is on a $140,000-a-year contract and Hickey has a $100,000

Lanny McDonald leaving ice after Leafs practice—minutes later he learned that he had been traded to Colorado. (Ron Bull/Toronto Star)

"If you don't look beyond the straight hockey aspect of it, it is a good trade but beyond that, it's the most classless thing I've ever hear of."

pact. McDonald is on a $149,000 contract, Quenneville an estimated $75,000.

It was the second Toronto trade in two days. Thursday, Leafs dealt veteran winger Pat Boutette to Hartford Whalers for utility forward Bob Stephenson.

Attorney Al Eagleson, who represents all but Hickey among the principals in the trade, considered the trade a good one for all involved.

"If you don't look beyond the straight hockey aspect of it, it is a good trade but beyond that, it's the most classless thing I've ever hear of," he said.

"Paiement's wife is expecting within four hours and McDonald's wife is due in January. Besides that, Lanny just bought a new home."

While the players were surprised at the trade, Eagleson wasn't.

"Other general managers told me Imlach had offered McDonald and when they asked about Sittler, he told them the deal (the $500,000 price tag on buying out Sittler's no-trade clause). He wasn't going to pay it so the guy taking Darryl would have had to."

Eagleson wasn't around the Gardens yesterday but he correctly imagined what the players were saying.

"There'll be a parade of players wanting out of there now," he predicted.

Mind you, what the players were saying came in the heat of the moment. Only time will tell whether the trade was a good one or not.

And only time will tell when the next Leaf trade will be made. ●

Vaive Tops Big M's Record

Captain's 49th Goal Breaks 21-Year-Old Mark

By Frank Orr • Published: March 25, 1982

In many ways, Rick Vaive represents a mistake of the type the Maple Leafs can't afford to make if their plans to reconstruct the club with young players is to be successful.

Vaive scored four goals last night in the Leafs' 8–5 victory over Chicago Black Hawks at Maple Leaf Gardens, giving him 49 for the season, a team record, breaking the standard of 48, established by Frank Mahovlich in the 1960–61 season.

If the Leafs' rebuilding program is to pay off, they simply can't give up on young players too soon as Vancouver Canucks did with Vaive in the 1979–80 season, when he was halfway through his rookie National Hockey League season.

That reversed a trend in recent Leaf history. They've lost patience with several young players over the years, traded them away and watched them become good NHL workers with other clubs.

Punch Imlach, Leaf general manger at the time, made what has turned out to be a superb deal when he secured Vaive and centre Bill Derlago from the Canucks in February of 1980 for Tiger Williams and Jerry Butler.

Butler is now in the minors; Williams has scored 15 goals for the Canucks this season.

The Canucks had picked Vaive, at 19, as their first-round selection in the '79 entry draft from Birmingham Bulls of the old World Hockey Association. The Vancouver club officials claimed Vaive reported to training camp out of shape and didn't have the most devoted attitude they had encountered.

"It was a big blow when the Canucks traded me," Vaive said.

"I was 20 years old and single and, sure, I had a little fun. But I wasn't any worse than a great many guys. I still like to enjoy myself.

"But I felt that I could play in the NHL if I got the chance. The Leafs gave it to me."

Now, Vaive and Derlago are the cornerstones of the Leaf plans for the future. At 22, Vaive is the big gunner, the hard-striding winger with the big shot, who was named the club captain on an interim basis after Darryl Sittler bolted the team in January.

"If anything, wearing the C helped me overcome a tendency to let down occasionally or, at least, the number of times I did because I felt that I had to supply some leadership," he said.

"I'd trade a few of my goals for about 15 more points in the standings because that would give us a playoff spot."

Vaive feels the Leafs are on the right track to respectability.

"I'd trade a few of my goals for about 15 more points in the standings because that would give us a playoff spot." Vaive said. "Sure this hasn't been the greatest season, but we're heading in the right direction. I think the club has a group of young players now who are going to be good ones when they get some experience. We have a good skating team and plenty of size.

"I think the future is very bright for this team."

"Vaive is the type of young player who's going to turn things around for this team," said Leaf coach Mike Nykoluk. "Guys like Rick give this team a good future, if we're all around to see it pay off."

There has been considerable speculation that Leaf owner Harold Ballard plans to replace Nykoluk as Leaf coach.

An interesting footnote last night was the fact that Mahovlich and Bobby Hull, who broke into the NHL with the Leafs and Hawks in '57–58 and finished 1–2 in the voting for the top rookie award, lost their club records on the same evening.

The Hawks' brilliant second-year centre, Denis Savard, picked up three assists to lift his point total to 110 and break Hull's mark of 107, set in '68–69.

The Leafs postponed the inevitable with their victory last night. With six games to play in the season, they trail the Black Hawks by 11 points for fourth place in the Norris Division and a spot in the Stanley Cup playoffs. A Leaf loss or a Hawk victory mathematically eliminates Toronto from Cup competition.

It was a big night for another Leaf, defenceman Barry Melrose, who scored his first goal of the season. He also has four assists.

"I had been tied with Bunny Larocque (Leaf goalie) on the scoring list at three assists," Melrose said. "Then I inched ahead with an assist and that goal means that I've blown old Bunny right out of the picture."

John Anderson, Dan Maloney and Rocky Saganiuk had the other Leaf goals.

Anderson was taken to the hospital, suffering from a hyper-extension (whiplash) of his neck when he collided with two Hawks. However, the injury isn't serious.

Doug Crossman, Tom Lysiak, Darryl Sutter, Glen Sharpley and Doug Wilson had the Black Hawk goals. ●

Rick Vaive scored his 50th goal vs. St. Louis just days after netting his team-record 49th goal vs. Chicago. He finished the 1981–82 season with 54 goals. (Dick Darrell/Toronto Star)

Wendel Clark Is No. 1 Pick in Draft

Leafs Take Young Defenceman but He Might Play on the Wing

By Frank Orr • Published: June 16, 1985

Wendel Clark and Craig Simpson were the first two players selected in yesterday's National Hockey League entry draft. Clark was surprised when he became a Maple Leaf; Simpson seemed relieved when he didn't.

The Leafs picked Clark, 18, a defenceman from Saskatoon Blades who also has played left wing, as the first selection in the draft, the club's reward for a last place over-all finish last season.

Simpson, a centre at Michigan State University who was rated as the No. 1 prospect in the draft by the NHL's Central Scouting Bureau, was the second choice, snapped up happily by Pittsburgh Penguins.

At one time, the Penguins considered offering the Leafs a player in a trade to guarantee that the Toronto club wouldn't take Simpson but, as it turned out, that wasn't necessary.

Many NHL folks figured that the Leafs would claim defenceman Dana Murzyn of Calgary Wranglers, who was rated No. 2 on the CSB list. However, he was the fifth pick by Hartford Whalers after New Jersey Devils picked defenceman Craig Wolanin of Kitchener Rangers third and Vancouver Canucks claimed winger Jim Sandlak of London Nights as the No. 4 pick.

General Manager Gerry McNamara said that the Leafs didn't decide on which of the three players—Simpson, Clark and Murzyn—they would claim as No. 1 until Friday night. It appears that some extremely edgy discussions with Simpson and his family—the differences were resolved partially last week—and the Leafs' need for aid immediately placed Clark at the head of their list.

The majority of NHL tam ratings showed there was little to choose between Clark and Simpson as prospects but Clark was the player in the draft most capable of playing in the NHL immediately.

Clark prefers to play defence but simply wants to play in the NHL at any position. The Leafs gave him no guarantees as to their plans

18-year-old Wendel Clark with Harold Ballard after he was taken first over-all in the 1985 NHL entry draft.
(Rick Eglinton/Toronto Star)

"It was a big surprise when the Leafs claimed me but I'm happy that they did."

for him but their personnel situation indicates he could be deployed as a winger, the spot he was working when he scored the goal against Czechoslovakia that gave the Canadian team this year's world junior championship.

"It was a big surprise when the Leafs claimed me but I'm happy that they did," Clark said. "I think of myself as a defenceman but I'll go to training camp with an open mind."

The book on Clark says he has strong skill in fundamentals, skating, shooting and passing, is tough and aggressive and plays with abundant enthusiasm, the latter a quality the Leafs need.

Perhaps Clark's value was confirmed when New York Islanders, a top team in the evaluation of talent, made a pitch for the Leaf's No. 1 choice, offering their two first-rounders (Nos. 6 and 13). They would have used the pick to take Clark.

A native of Kelvington, Sask., where his family farms more than 3,000 acres, with 2,900 acres of grain planted this spring, Clark is a cousin of former Leafs defenceman Barry Melrose.

Simpson insisted that being picked by the Leafs would not have been the end of the world.

"But I was a little unsure of Toronto's plans for me and I felt a little more comfortable with the Penguins," said Simpson, who has completed two years of college studies. "Also, I want to continue my education and my college credits are much more portable than if I switched to a Canadian school."

Other draft picks by the Leafs were defenceman Ken Spangler from Calgary, left winger Dave Thomlinson from Brandon Wheat Kings, Peterborough centre Greg Vey, defenceman Jeff Serowik of Lawrence Academy in New Hampshire, Czech defenceman Jiri Latal, North Bay winger Tim Bean, centre Andy Donahue from Belmont, Mass., centre Todd Whittemore of Kent School in Taunton, Mass., centre Bob Reynolds from St. Clair Shores, Marlboro centre Tim Armstrong and goalie Mitch Murphy from St. Paul, Minn.

The Sabres claimed Windsor centre Keith Gretzky, the brother of Edmonton's great Wayne Gretzky, on the third round, the 56th player picked. Keith, who is 5-foot-9 and weighs 157 pounds, improved dramatically over the past season and has started a weight-training program to increase his weight. ●

'Too Tough to Play under Those Conditions'

Leeman Outspoken as Coach Brophy Fired

By Randy Starkman • Published: December 20, 1988

The way Gary Leeman views it, John Brophy's iron-fisted rule over the Toronto Maple Leafs made the team too tense to play winning hockey.

Most of the players chose to stick to platitudes in the wake of Brophy's firing yesterday. They said they felt sorry for the coach, that they were just as much to blame and that hard work would turn things around.

But Leeman took a more forthright approach. He said most of the players had lost their confidence because of Brophy's constant harangues.

"It's come to the point now where guys throw the puck around and are afraid it's going to hop over their sticks," said Leeman. "That's the feeling you get. It's too tough to play under those conditions. It's not fair to the team to play under those conditions."

Leeman said the players and their volatile coach just weren't on the same wavelength.

"I think it came down to management making a decision on the chemistry of this team and maybe the conflict between John and the players," he said. "There were a lot of things changing, a lot of things up in the air, a lot of indirection.

"I think that's probably why John's not coaching now. The chemistry wasn't there. I don't know whether the game has passed John by or not. I know deep down that he cared. The thing about it is some things on a person-to-person basis were difficult for him to handle."

The sixth-year player said Brophy had a tendency to dwell too much on the negative.

"You've got to be able to realize why you lost; you've got to be able to accept it when it happens; and you've got to be able to instill things in a positive way that are going to help the team....I know there were a lot of cases when the team became too tense to play."

Brophy narrowly escaped the axe last season, as the team barely squeaked into the playoffs and the players seemed to verge on mutiny. But the coach toned his approach down this year and the Leafs got off to a sizzling 8–3–1 start.

"If you look where we were last year at the end of April, the fact we started September without a lynching I think is a success in itself."

Unfortunately for Brophy, it didn't last long. And as the team's fortunes began to deteriorate on the ice, so did his relationship with the players off it.

"If you look where we were last year at the end of April, the fact we started September without a lynching I think is a success in itself," said Toronto GM Gord Stellick. "I think Brophy deserves a lot of credit for improving relations with the team initially and getting things going.

"But when things started to go into a skid, it's like a bad relationship. When you get back together again and things go sour again, it just drops to rock bottom right away."

It has been suggested that some players gave less than a full effort in order to expedite Brophy's firing, but Leeman said he didn't put much stock in that theory.

"I would hate to believe that some of my teammates were thinking like that," he said. "I don't think that happened."

Ed Olczyk said several Leafs dogged it last year in the hope that Brophy would be fired, but ex-general manager Gerry McNamara was sacked instead.

"It happened last year and nothing happened (to Brophy) and I seriously doubt that anyone was doing it this year," said Olczyk. "John was totally different this year, a complete turnaround, but we still had the same result and we, as players, have to take a lot of the blame."

Olczyk said it wasn't a case of the players losing faith in Brophy.

"I think we lost confidence in one another," he said. "When you go 10 games and don't win, that's hard. It's tough to go home, tough to go to the local grocery store. It's not easy, especially in a place like this."

Veteran winger Al Secord said a number of factors were involved, the key one being that the Leafs are not playing well as a unit.

"I think it was a combination of a little bit of tension, a lack of confidence, just some guys not going well, some guys going well. Everybody's playing in different directions. I think most of the guys are playing to the best of their ability, but we're not playing as one."

Defenceman Brian Curran, who has been given a heavy workload this season, prospered under Brophy. He had nothing but praise for him.

"He was a winner, that's all I can say about John," said Curran. "He wanted to win, tried his best to win, did the things he thought necessary to win. Maybe we didn't respond to it as well as we should have." ●

Leafs started well under coach John Brophy in 1988 but then things quickly went downhill.
(Andrew Stawicki/Toronto Star)

Return to Respectability

The 90s begin badly as the Leafs lose one division semi-final and then miss the playoffs for two straight seasons but everything changes when General Manager Cliff Fletcher pulls off what many regard as the best trade in the team's history

FAST FACTS

- Defenceman Al Iafrate is sent to Washington on January 16, 1991 in a deal that brings centre Peter Zezel to Toronto.

- Cliff Fletcher is hired as president and general manager of the Leafs on July 1, 1991, succeeding Gerry McNamara. A year later he fires coach Tom Watt and hires Pat Burns.

- Leafs land high-scoring winger Dave Andreychuk on February 2, 1993 in a deal that sends goaltender Grant Fuhr to Buffalo. He scores 53 goals during the 1993–94 season and eventually wins a Stanley Cup—but with Tampa Bay.

- Draft pick Felix Potvin takes over as the team's No. 1 goalie in 1992 and backstops to team to 160 wins over the next seven seasons, third most in Leafs' history behind Tuck Broda and Johnny Bower.

- Doug Gilmour sets two team records during the 1992-93 season with 127 points and 93 assists. Both records still stand.

- Defenceman Borje Salming, who spent 16 seasons in a Leafs uniform, is elected to the Hockey Hall of Fame in September 1996. He scored 147 goals and had 620 assists over 1099 games beginning in 1973 before being traded to Detroit in 1989.

- Ken Dryden takes over as president and general manager of the team in 1997 and a year later fires coach Mike Murphy.

- Mats Sundin, named captain before the 1997-98 season, leads by example as he tops the Leafs in scoring in 12 of his 13 seasons in Toronto (he was second to Alex Mogilny in 2002-03).

- Pat Quinn takes over behind the bench to begin the 1998-99 season and the Leafs finish with a 45-30-7 record before losing the conference final to Buffalo.

- Goaltender Curtis Joseph is signed as a free agent on July 15, 1998 and proceeds to lead the team into the playoffs for four straight seasons. He wins 138 regular season games in a Leafs uniform and another 32 playoff games.

Felix Potvin took over in the Leafs' nets in 1992 and led the team to four straight playoff appearances.
(Peter Power/Toronto Star)

'Killer' Breathes Life into Leafs

Gilmour Agrees to Multi-Year Contract

By Rosie DiManno • Published: February 1, 1992

When Doug Gilmour stepped onto the ice at the Saddledome on New Year's Eve, he knew it would be his last game as a Calgary Flame.

As swan songs go, it was a pretty aria. Calgary won that contest against the Montreal Canadiens in overtime. Gilmour counted one goal and one assist.

After it was over, the players celebrated and slapped bums at centre ice. The year was drawing rapidly to a close and there was a feeling in the air, in that joyful and sweaty arena, that the storm of discontent in Calgary had finally broken. It was an illusion.

Gilmour was bear hugged by his teammate, and neighbor, Gary Roberts. "I looked at him right there on the ice and I said, 'Well buddy, this is my last game tonight.' He said: 'I knew sooner or later it would be.'"

A team party followed, with the players and their wives and the bubbly flowing.

"We took a video camera to the party," recalls Gilmour's wife, Robyne. "We knew this would be the last time we'd be all together. I started to cry. Doug had this humongous lump in his throat.

But I know the whole situation was killing Doug. He just couldn't take it any more."

The next morning, Gilmour got to the rink early, packed up his things and walked out on the club.

For an athlete in a team sport, this can be considered the ultimate betrayal—putting self ahead of the rest, the individual ahead of the group.

As he was leaving, Gilmour ran into Doug Risebrough, the intransigent manager of the Flames and the man who had become the enemy. "He said, 'Doug, if you leave now I'm going to trade you.' I said, if he could resolve the situation, great. If not, I though it was fair to move on."

Less than 24 hours later, Doug Gilmour was traded to the Toronto Maple Leafs, the catalyst and featured act in an unprecedented 10-player swap that sent disgruntled Bud Gary Leeman in the opposite direction.

"Risebrough called me at home the next day. Said I'd been traded to Toronto. Nothing else, no details. I just said thank you and 'bye. Then I dropped the phone and ran leaping around the

Doug Gilmour signed a multi-year contract that paid about $1 million per season. (Rick Eglinton/Toronto Star)

"Riser and I had been going at it a long time," says Gilmour. "He wasn't going to give in to me and I wasn't going to give in to him. See, I think Risebrough and I are a lot alike. I think we were both kind of pig-headed."

house. If there was any place I wanted to go, it was Toronto."

A rather masochistic ambition, perhaps.

In truth, Gilmour figures he was on his way to Toronto "about 200 times in the last couple of years." At one time, when Cliff Fletcher was still calling the shots in Calgary, there were Doug Gilmour-for-Wendel Clark rumbles. When he landed in Toronto this year as grand poobah of all things blue and beautiful, Fletcher set about trying to finagle a deal that would put his former serf Gilmour in a Leaf yoke.

For Gilmour, who had been a key performer in the Flame ascendency of the late '80s—including their first Stanley Cup championship in 1989—there was nothing left in Calgary but acrimony and ill will.

The clash with Risebrough, Fletcher's protégé, is of long standing, says Gilmour's agent Larry Kelly. "The club had known all last year that there were serious personality problems between Doug and Risebrough."

But Kelly was not among those urging Gilmour to abandon the club, according to the player's wife. "His agent kept saying wait, wait. But I knew Doug couldn't wait much longer. It was obvious just by the way Risebrough would look at Doug on the bench. I could tell he had daggers in his eyes."

But why the brittle relationship in the first place? The genesis of the rancor is not altogether clear. Gilmour, however, is convinced that he was no longer a key component in the Flames plans for the future and that he was being treated as a marginal player. There was no respect.

"Calgary had six or seven good players but they also had a couple of young guys that they felt could possibly do the same kind of job that I was doing. They wanted another winger that could score and they wanted (Theo) Fleury back at centre. I knew the writing was on the wall."

So Gilmour wanted to be traded and he believed Risebrough was gratuitously thwarting those plans. Suddenly, it all become personal, very personal.

"Riser and I had been going at it a long time," says Gilmour. "He wasn't going to give in to me and I wasn't going to give in to him. See, I think Risebrough and I are a lot alike. I think we were both kind of pig-headed. We both said some things...."

The final straw was the arbitration decision last December that went against Gilmour. He had taken the Flames to salary arbitration, asking for $1.2 million (US). The club countered with an offer of $550,000. The arbitrator settled on $750,000.

"I could live with the decision about the money. But I was upset with the whole arbitration process. The way management picked (the arbitrator) up at the airport and sat with him at the game. Then we came in with 200 pages of arguments as far as what we wanted and Calgary came in with three pages.

"It's obvious that players are not going to get a fair decision in the NHL right now and that has to be changed through the NHL Players Association."

So, not long afterwards, Gilmour set aside all the principles with which he was raised and abandoned his hockey club.

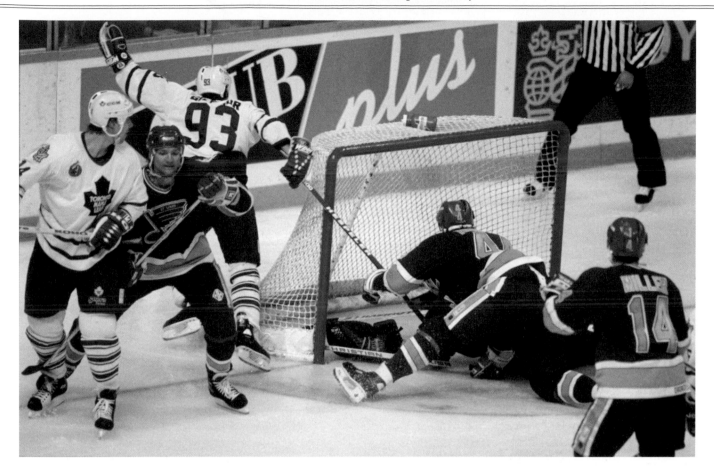

"Oh, they crucified me in the papers. Man, this was the toughest decision I've ever had to make in my lifetime. But I did not leave the team right before a game. There were four open days there to make a trade.

"I didn't quit."

Doug Gilmour is sitting in a downtown restaurant, tucking into a plate of pasta and sipping on a beer.

The afternoon hours are an idle time for a professional hockey player, especially one newly transplanted to a still-strange city. He has spent much of his free time looking for a house to rent so he can bring Robyne and six-year-old daughter Maddison to Toronto.

In the meantime, he is living in a hotel. Fortunately, he likes solitude.

There is a vaguely Satanic look to Gilmour, whose face is all dark planes and deep shadows. The eyes are intense and as black as cocoa beans. Around the league, they call him Killer, a moniker that was bestowed upon him years ago by Brian Sutter.

"He thought I looked like Charlie Manson. I don't know whether it fits or not. Killer is a hard name to live up to. Other players look at me and they see this little guy, 168 pounds, and they think: This is Killer?" He chortles contentedly.

There is much to be content about these days. This week, Gilmour agreed to terms on a multi-year contract with the Leafs that will pay him about $1 million a season.

Since coming to Toronto, Gilmour has given further proof to the general consensus that the Flames were royally bamboozled in The Big Trade. In the process, wing-mate Glenn Anderson has blossomed as well. And don't look now, but the Leafs are riding a three-game win streak at the moment, thanks largely to Gilmour and Anderson.

"I am just so happy to be here," says Gilmour, launching into the dutiful language of the working jock. "Glenn and I, we're still kind of reading each other. I like to drop the puck behind me and he can take the

Doug Gilmour was the key to the Leafs' 1993 playoff run, scoring the winning goal in overtime in Game 1 of the division semi-final vs. St. Louis. (Colin McConnell/Toronto Star)

puck to the net hard. He drives to the net. He's kind of courageous that way."

Gilmour's forte is as a playmaker, a tactician. His idol is Wayne Gretzky, who manages to be both a marksman and a selfless team player.

He is protective about the Leafs and impatient with those who would mock the club's overly modest accomplishments of the past, oh, quarter-century.

"I'm very defensive if somebody says something to me about the Toronto Maple Leafs. I don't know anything about what happened here in the past and I don't really care. Now it's just a matter of having a winning attitude. Every team needs confidence.

"Me? I'm just so excited about coming to a team that wanted me. I know hockey is a business but it has to be fun, too. And right now, it's a lot of fun."

There is a picture of Doug Gilmour that has somehow found a home for itself in the locker room stall of Calgary Flame Joe Nieuwendyk. It shows a little boy, just barely two years old, wearing a Montreal Canadiens jersey and standing wobbly-legged on tiny skates.

The picture was taken on a patch of ice in front of Gilmour's childhood home in Kingston. It is a snapshot of Canadiana. But on a smaller scale, it sums up the young Gilmour's hopes and dreams and ambitions. (Except for the still puzzling Montreal angle. Gilmour was a steadfast Boston Bruin fan.)

Gilmour is the youngest of five children. Big Brother David, 13 years older, was himself a one-time NHL prospect who played with Darryl Sittler on the London Knights and had a brief sojourn with Calgary in the World Hockey Association.

"He's a hockey player and that's what I wanted to be from Day One. But he was so much older, he had already moved away by the time I started playing. My dad was my real teacher."

His dad was also, for 32 years, the storage keeper at Kingston Penitentiary. The Gilmours were a penal-oriented family. Mom Dolly worked at the Staff College and Joyceville Penitentiary. Sister Debbie is a guard at the women's penitentiary. For a time, David was a recreational worker at Millhaven though he now tends bar at a Kingston saloon. (Another sister, Donna, is married to a former Vancouver Canuck who now plays in Austria.)

"I was a real small kid," recalls Gilmour. "One of those little brats. I didn't play any school sports. My mind was just hockey, hockey, hockey. Every day after class, I couldn't wait to get home and play on the street."

It was grit, as well as a natural talent, that got Gilmour noticed and promoted up the echelons of organized hockey. When he was 17 he left home to play as a junior with the Cornwall Royals.

"You grow up fast in this game. Hockey takes a lot away from you when you're a teenager. Your friends, your home life. I quit school early too, only got my Grade 12 and that's something I regret. That's one thing I hope to do this summer, go back to school and take some classes."

In particular, he would like to study broadcasting or acting, though he's a little bashful about talking about the latter. Last year, it was announced that a Hollywood producer had taken out a $5 million life insurance policy on Gilmour, who was going to star in a movie about the late race car driver, Peter Revson. The scheme fell through but there is still a possibility that Gilmour will be cast in a small role as Jesse James in another film under consideration.

"It's all entertainment, isn't it?" asks Gilmour, rhetorically. "I'm in an entertainment business right now."

It was in Cornwall restaurant one night that Gilmour, celebrating a consecutive point streak of 55 games, met a young nursing student called Robyne who was four years his senior and knew absolutely nothing about hockey. "He was so cute and quiet," recalls Robynne. They were married within a year. Gilmour was only 20.

"All of a sudden you're making $80,000, you've got a nice car and all this freedom. I didn't know whether I would have enough common sense or enough self-control to keep myself out of trouble. Getting married seemed the smart thing to do."

"I remember the day he told me that he had been drafted by the St. Louis Blues," says Robyne. "I thought he meant he'd been drafted into the army! I didn't have a clue what he was talking about but I just kept

"All of a sudden you're making $80,000, you've got a nice car and all this freedom. I didn't know whether I would have enough common sense or enough self-control to keep myself out of trouble. Getting married seemed the smart thing to do."

nodding my head because I didn't want him to think that I was stupid."

After being voted the Ontario Hockey League's outstanding player in his final year, Gilmour was bitterly disappointed with his seventh-round draft selection. Disenchanted with the Blues' offer, he fled to West Germany to check out the hockey action but he was lured back within days.

In 1983, Gilmour embarked on an admirable career with the Blues. Life was sweet in St. Louis both on and off the ice. But in 1988, everything disintegrated in a very public and very ugly manner.

The parents of a 14-year-old girl who occasionally baby-sat Maddison accused Gilmour of having sexual relations with the teen. They claimed the carnal relationship was known both to Gilmour's wife and his employers.

The story made major headlines. There were reports at the time that the Blues had made hush-hush payments to the family. Gilmour categorically refutes those allegations.

What got smaller play were subsequent stories that a grand jury declined to indict Gilmour on the charges. The family then launched a $1 million civil suit. Gilmour countersued. Meanwhile, with everyone agreeing it was the right thing to do, Gilmour was traded in the offseason to the Flames.

Gilmour is still reluctant to discuss the whole sordid mess, especially with the civil suits still pending. But he acknowledges the toll that the experience took on his professional and personal life. "I don't want to say anything bad about anybody. I don't want to talk about what may have motivated the family." Like extortion, for instance, which is more common with athletes than the public realizes.

"There was no truth to the charges and no evidence. But people don't remember that part. You learn a lot about yourself. You've got to be strong. You learn who you can trust. It makes you very cautious. It was hard for my wife, of course. She had to ask me the question, didn't she? She had to ask her husband if he had done this thing.

"But, truthfully, it brought us a lot closer. We came through it."

And Doug Gilmour has come through a lot more since then. ●

Burns Takes Charge

Love Him, Hate Him—Former Hab Mentor Is a First-Rate Coach

By Bob McKenzie • Published: May 30, 1992

It was the last day of 1991 and Pat Burns was in the lobby of a Calgary hotel, doing what he does best.

Talking.

Now, Burns is a pretty fair National Hockey League coach. Some would even suggest he's as good as there is. But as well as he matches wits behind the bench, the 22nd man to guide the fortunes of the Toronto Maple Leafs can talk to beat the band. Banal, he isn't.

His language is colorful—mostly blue—and has the edge of the tough street kid that he was while growing up in St-Henri, one of the poorest neighborhoods in all of Montreal.

"Hey, maybe I should be working in Toronto, eh?" he said last New Year's Eve.

It was hard to tell just how serious he was. It was said in the most lighthearted fashion possible. But it certainly wasn't the first time he had broached the subject.

When Mike Keenan, Brian Sutter, Tom Webster, Tom Watt and Burns formed the Canada Cup coaching equivalent of the glee club last fall, he playfully envisioned himself working in Hogtown. A couple of months later, on a road trip to New York and with his Habs the toast of the NHL, he quipped with Toronto reporters there about what it would be like to be the head coach of the Maple Leafs.

Now, he's going to find out.

Leaf general manager Cliff Fletcher announced yesterday that Burns will succeed Tom Watt as the club's head coach.

Maybe nothing in this business should come as a surprise any more, not after the trading of Wayne Gretzky anyway, but Burns as coach of the Leafs is a shock to the system.

Actually, the surprise isn't Burns being named coach of the Leafs so much as it is him no longer being coach of the Canadiens.

The 40-year-old former cop was born to be a Hab. Or so it seemed.

The youngest of six children to an anglophone father, Albert, and a francophone mother, Louise, he grew up not too far from the venerable Forum.

"My mother couldn't speak English and my father couldn't speak French," he said, "but they must have been able to communicate because they made six of us kids."

He said it wasn't all that long ago that he paid scalpers for tickets to see Scott Bowman coach Guy Lafleur and Larry Robinson.

Pat Burns was a blue-collar coach who believed in taking care of defence. (John Mahler/Toronto Star)

He's a hard-bitten disciplinarian, the ex-cop who did everything from undercover work (bushy beard and hair way down his back) to homicide investigations to breaking up barroom brawls and handing out parking tickets.

Suddenly, it was he who had ascended to the same office as legends like Toe Blake and Bowman.

There was, of course, a 17-year career as a police officer and detective, mostly in Gatineau, just across the river from Ottawa; four years as coach of the Hull Olympiques; and one year with Montreal's farm team in Sherbrooke.

And now, after four winning NHL seasons, one Stanley Cup appearance, one coach-of-the-year award and more causes celebres in Montreal than he cares to count, he voluntarily surrenders it all to work in the bastion of anglo Canada.

Go figure.

Burns got tired of life in what he calls "the toughest job in hockey." Many of those around him grew weary of his act, too, though they were prepared to have him carry on next season anyway.

Ironic as it may be, a man whose lineage is half French-Canadian, half Irish couldn't cope with the duality that goes with being coach of Les Canadiens.

In many respects, Burns was never accepted by the influential francophone media of Montreal. And he never accepted them either.

In any case, it was a strained relationship from start to finish. Fluently bilingual, they mocked the roughness of his French, which he never really learned to speak until he was 16.

He had celebrated run-ins with local heroes Stephane Richer, Claude Lemieux and Stephan Lebeau, among others. He was even branded as anti-French, a notion he dismissed as ludicrous.

He did, however, concede to be anti-flake, and when Richer and Lemieux, for example, drove him crazy with their temperamental ways, he, in concert with Hab GM Serge Savard, saw that they were traded away.

Burns is the embodiment of Gallic pride and Irish temper, a lethal combination. He professed to be tougher than his many Montreal critics—make no mistake, he is one tough SOB and plays the role to the hilt—but it was they who finally wore him down. To suggest otherwise is to deny he's now a Maple Leaf.

Burns is a man of many faces.

He's a country music buff who plays guitar and sings.

He's an incurable practical joker with a true zest for life.

He's a hard-bitten disciplinarian, the ex-cop who did everything from undercover work (bushy beard and hair way down his back) to homicide investigations to breaking up barroom brawls and handing out parking tickets.

He claims never to read newspapers but those who know him say he reads every sentence, word, comma and period.

He is deeply committed to his work, first as a police officer and now as a coach and has the failed marriage to prove it.

His claim to fame, though, is as a blue-collar coach who believes in taking care of defence first and putting his motivational message over to his players like so few others in the game can.

His Habs were a model of consistency, either the first- or second-best defensive club in each of Burns' four years in Montreal.

Yet he himself has undergone a significant meta-morphosis since being in the NHL.

With each passing year, he has become more outspoken and colorful, more self-assured and, at times, more outrageous than perhaps he has a right to be.

He is titillated by colorful and controversial coaches in the National Football League, such as Atlanta's Jerry Glanville, and talks about the art of the news conference and how to give the media what it is they want most—controversy.

He hasn't disappointed.

Burns can be both politically and socially incorrect, which is either refreshing or revolting, depending upon personal sensitivities.

When Hab bad boy Shayne Corson got in yet another barroom incident this season, Burns went on French-language radio and said, "As far as I'm concerned, Shayne Corson can eat s---."

L'Actualite, the French-language version of Maclean's magazine, did a question-and-answer interview session with him covering a broad range of topics, everything from the war in Iraq to homosexuality in the NHL. Honest to a fault, Burns said he wouldn't feel comfortable with a known homosexual on his hockey team. It didn't sit well in some quarters.

Even some of his biggest boosters thought him too full of himself this year; that he spoke first and thought later; that he lost some of his effectiveness with his players and became too enamored of hearing his own voice. Also, that he was more interested in disposing of problems (Richer, Lemieux et al) than solving them.

He is liable to say just about anything, as was the case for a story that appeared this season in Inside HOCKEY magazine, relating to the fractious political scene in Quebec and Canada.

"I love the culture in Quebec," he is quoted as saying. "And I think we're getting a bad rap in the rest of Canada....The last thing I want is for Quebec to separate. I'm as proud a Canadian as they come. But I think Quebec is just trying to protect its culture. I don't know how to say this without getting into trouble, but how many white faces do you see in downtown Toronto any more?"

Leave it to Burns to defend Quebec's distinct society by taking a shot at Toronto's multiculturalism. That doesn't necessarily make him racist—he's an equal opportunity employer so long as the guy has defensive tendencies—but it does make him someone who, as he proclaims, often doesn't know how to say something "without getting into trouble."

He could choose to say nothing, but then he wouldn't be true to himself and he couldn't live with that either.

None of this, though, should obscure Fletcher's point in bringing Burns to Toronto.

As a coach, and even as a person, too, Burns' assets so far outweigh any liabilities that it's no contest.

That's what made yesterday such an exciting day for the Maple Leaf franchise. Not since Punch Imlach, in his first tour of duty back in the '50s and '60s, has the club had a coach with the presence of Burns.

It is difficult not to be excited at what's happening on Carlton Street. For too many years now, Leaf fans have had to be content with the game's bit players—on and off the ice.

Many of them committed the cardinal sins of being both incompetent and boring.

Fletcher has changed all that. He's running the Leafs like the first-class operation it should have been and surrounding himself with some stars and strong personalities, from Grant Fuhr to Bill Watters to Doug Gilmour and now Pat Burns.

There's never any telling what the end result will be—there are no guarantees in sport—but the Leafs finally look to be on the right track. The hiring of Burns could put them on the fast track, too.

All things considered, Pat Burns is a good guy, salt of the earth you might say.

More importantly, though, he is an excellent coach who, in spite of his gift of the gab, does more than talk a good game. ●

Dream Season Comes to a Crashing End

But Gilmour, Clark Redefine Maple Leaf Pride

By Bob McKenzie • Published: May 30, 1993

Wayne Gretzky was grand. Simply marvelous.

But were Doug Gilmour and Wendel Clark any less so?

Perhaps, but only in increments unmeasured by man.

The Los Angeles Kings' centre did in the Toronto Maple Leaf season last night the way he's done in so many teams before—stealing the show at centre stage with the spotlight firmly on him.

His stick was a stiletto, carving up the Leafs with a precision so few, if any, can match when the opportunistic one is on his game.

Three goals and one assist to the lead the Kings to their 5-4 win and put Los Angeles in the Stanley Cup final against Montreal for the very first time.

Unbelievable.

But Gilmour and Clark were anything but in the shadows. No supporting roles for them.

The Leafs' Dream Season came to a crushing end last night, but not for lack of effort by men of extraordinary character and courage.

All the Leaf players deserve to take a bow, but there would not have been a dream season if not for Gilmour, who from start to finish has been the Leafs' heart and soul. And when the games meant the most this spring, Clark was right there with him.

Killer and the Captain.

Clark had two goals last night, Gilmour three assists. The numbers, though, don't even begin to do justice to their efforts in Game 7 against the Kings and, for that matter, throughout this most incredible of springs.

"We played 21 games in 42 nights," Leafs' coach Pat Burns said. "I've never been more proud of a team than I am right now. And that's exactly what I told them."

He was asked specifically about Gilmour and Clark.

"Doug Gilmour is the most valuable player I've had anything to do with, he just did it all for us," Burns said. "I know Wendel has had some ups and maybe a couple of downs, he showed a lot of leadership during these playoffs and scored big goals."

The Leafs fell into a hole early last night and Gilmour was as much responsible as anyone. It was his power-play pass that was intercepted by Jari Kurri, who started the play that was finished with Gretzky's game-opening shorthanded goal.

And Gilmour was on the ice, pressing deep as he always does, when the Kings turned it back up for Tomas Sandstrom's goal, set up by Gretzky.

Redemption came swiftly.

First, Gilmour set up Clark for a Leaf power-play goal early in the second period. Then, Gilmour battled little Corey Millen to feed the puck to another playoff warrior, Glenn Anderson, who rifled it past netminder Kelly Hrudey.

Gretzky restored the Kings' lead in the second period, but Gilmour, the passer, and Clark, the shooter, combined once again early in the third to tie the game.

A couple of bad bounces led to the Leafs' demise—first on Mike Donnelly's marker and then Gretzky's third of the game—but even then they weren't finished.

Gilmour and Clark led the charge in the final two minutes, resulting in Dave Ellett's goal at 18:53.

The final harried minute of the Leaf season was spent almost entirely in the Kings' end, with Clark waging war in the corners and in front of the net and Gilmour desperately trying to deal from behind the net.

He flailed valiantly to try to get the puck in front of the net, falling to the ice and picking himself back up again and again.

Teammates rush to embrace Wayne Gretzky after his third goal of the game gave the Kings a 5-4 win in Game 7 of the conference final. (Colin McConnell /Toronto Star)

It just wasn't to be. It was not a fitting end, for Gilmour and his team.

"It's disappointing, " Gilmour said. "It's frustrating. It's disappointing. We're not satisfied.

"There is a lot of character on this team. Lots of guts and determination. On paper, maybe this team doesn't look as good as some, but we have a work ethic and a coach who demands a lot of us. Beyond that, there's nothing else to say. Nothing."

Well, actually there is.

For far too long, being a Maple Leaf hasn't meant much.

That is, until Gilmour arrived last season and picked up the whole club, carrying it on his back and re-defining Maple Leaf pride and tradition along the way.

And what of Wendel, who so many of us were looking to ship out of town. He had his heart and soul questioned, but just pressed on, the epitome of true grit.

Clark not a Leaf? Perish the thought now.

"I just kept telling this team to kick at the darkness until the daylight shines through," Burns said. "It's sad. I feel for everyone in that room.

"But everyone knows now that if you're going to put on this (Maple Leaf) sweater, you better be ready to play."

Yes, the Leafs lost. But this edition of the Leafs, led by Gilmour and Clark in the playoffs, have re-established some very special."

They set a new standard for what it means to be a Maple Leaf.

The Maple Leaf warriors' only failing was that a guy named Gretzky re-discovered an old one. ●

Dejected Leafs Glenn Anderson, Kent Manderville, Nick Foligno, Wendel Clark and Dave Ellett after their loss to Los Angeles. (Ron Bull/Toronto Star)

Leafs Trade Captain Clark

Sundin Coming to Toronto Is Six-Player Deal

By Damien Cox • Published: June 29, 1994

At 2:55 p.m. yesterday, Cliff Fletcher didn't want to trade captain Wendel Clark.

At 3 p.m., he decided he had to.

With the Maple Leaf organization still reeling from the tragic death of head scout Pierre Dorion only three days earlier, Fletcher decided that the emotionally charged trading of Clark was the only way to ensure that the Maple Leafs would not degenerate into an old, spent hockey club in three or four years.

"But it was extremely hard, unbelievably hard," Fletcher said. "Wendel is Wendel. I just love the guy."

In a monster deal that had its seeds in a failed transaction between the Leafs and Nordiques at the March trading deadline, the two clubs rocked the Hartford Civic Centre and the hockey world an hour into the entry draft yesterday by consummating a six-player trade that also involved two first-round draft picks.

The Leafs sent Clark, rearguard Sylvain Lefebvre and University of North Dakota winger Landon Wilson to Quebec City in exchange for talented centre Mats Sundin, rugged blueliner Garth Butcher and Canadian Olympic team winger Todd Warriner.

Clark, whose name has been a staple in trade rumors for years, seemed resigned to the fact that a deal was inevitable.

"I know enough people around the game and I'd heard a lot things so it's not that much of a surprise," he told The Star's Paul Hunter.

"I'm disappointed to be leaving, I never wanted to leave Toronto but in today's game moving around is a big part of it. I'll just go to training camp and play hockey in another city."

The Toronto captain, often a reticent interview subject, even poked fun at himself as he fielded questions from a handful of reporters in front of his Madison Ave. home.

"I'm just being vague right now...like normal," he said, laughing. "I haven't talked to anyone in Quebec or with Toronto yet and I haven't really thought about things so I don't want to say too much. I'll have more to do in a day or two."

Clark spent yesterday filming a breakfast cereal commercial in Toronto. Fortunately, he said, he wasn't wearing a Maple Leaf sweater in the ad.

As he talked a stretch white limousine, with one-time Leaf now Winnipeg Jet Tie Domi sipping a beer in the backseat, sat idling on the driveway.

"I'll be everywhere," he said, when asked what his plans were for last evening. "I booked (the limo) about half an hour ago because I figured I wouldn't be able to drive home."

Clark said he'd be holding a press conference either today or tomorrow to discuss his feelings about his years in Toronto, the trade and the fans here.

The Leafs also traded the 22nd pick over-all to the Nords for the 10th selection in hopes of landing Kingston Frontenacs winger Brett Lindros. When that was foiled by another deal between the Nords and the New York Islanders, the Leafs traded the 10th pick

and the rights to free agent winger Rob Pearson to Washington for the 16th pick and multi-purpose centre Mike Ridley.

"It was the busiest day I've had since I came to Toronto," Fletcher said. "I don't think we'll be as good a team October 1st, but I'm hoping by March we'll be a better team."

While the loss of Clark and Pearson opens holes on the wing for the Leafs, the addition of Sundin, 23, and Ridley, 31, immediately solves the club's centre ice woes.

"Three hours ago the Leafs needed a second line centre," said Capitals GM David Poile. "They've clearly filled that void."

"We are definitely stronger down the middle," said head coach Pat Burns. "But I sure hated to give up a guy like Wendel. He's been a part of the Toronto Maple Leafs for a long time."

The 6-foot-2 Sundin, the No. 1 selection of the 1989 draft, is generally rated as one of the most skilled young players in hockey and now inherits the role as Doug Gilmour's successor as the club's No. 1 centre.

Still, most hockey observers were stunned that the Leafs chose to deal Clark.

"Toronto got by far the most talented guy, but Wendel was a great leader and great in the play-offs," said Chicago Blackhawk head coach Darryl Sutter. "I'm sure a lot of guys on our team are happy he's out of the division."

In Sundin, the Leafs have also inherited a possible contract problem. He has three years left on a five-year, $4 million contract he signed two years ago, but he has been anxious to renegotiate ever since the Nords signed Swedish youngster Peter Forsberg.

"(Sundin) was happy in Quebec, but the contract was a source of frustration for him," said Sundin's agent, Mark Perrone. "Because of that, he lost his focus a bit and didn't have a tremendous season. I haven't had a chance to talk to Toronto about any parameters as far as his contract.

"I don't know how he'll react to the trade, but I think he'll take it as a professional."

Sundin is scheduled to earn $900,000 this year, then $1.1 million and $1.3 million in the final years of his deal.

Clark said he expected he'd report to Quebec, "but I haven't even thought about those kinds of things." ●

Maple Leafs captain Wendel Clark was traded to Quebec for talented centre Mats Sundin. (David Cooper/Toronto Star)

Goodbye Gardens

Fans Weep as Hockey Era Ends

By Rosie DiManno • Published: February 14, 1999

Memories are not forever.

They fade, recede, become all jumbly and tangled and unreliable.

Years from now, how many thousands of fans, scores of thousands, will claim to have been at Maple Leaf Gardens on the evening of Feb. 13, 1999, for the last hurrah, the final farewell?

The false claimants will not be lying, not entirely. Just as I have almost convinced myself that I was in the building when the Toronto Maple Leafs last won the Stanley Cup in 1967, so others may come to believe they were present last night, when they spin their tales of reminiscence.

Twenty-four-thousand, five hundred and twenty-two nights earlier, the newly hatched Gardens had opened to the delight of a city that was not much more than a big town, stratified by class and colour and creed. Before a crowd of gentlemen in fedoras and bejeweled ladies in furs, the Leafs lost 2-1 to the Chicago Black Hawks.

Sixty-seven years and a bit later, the slightly rechristened Chicago Blackhawks returned to help close out an era. And these young Leafs, perhaps twitchy at the magnitude of the occasion, couldn't redeem themselves for that original defeat, which would at least

have provided some historical symmetry in the annals of the franchise. It was the 769th time they've lost at the Gardens.

Toronto lost 6-2, which was altogether embarrassing, and elicited a final round of jeers from the less sentimentally inclined.

And that's that. Bookended by the Blackhawks.

Seems like old times, indeed.

"This edition of the team has great heart and they wanted to win tonight, very badly, but we didn't do it," coach Pat Quinn noted, apologetically.

Tie Domi was equally regretful. "We're disappointed and we're sorry we let everybody down."

The lopsided outcome just made those bitter tears shed by fans a bit more legitimate. Regulars started crying, oh, 'round about the middle of the second period. By the time Curtis Joseph conceded the sixth goal—egad! Bob Probert scored the last NHL goal in the Gardens—they were verily sobbing, or hee-hawing.

This game counted in the standings, of course, more's the pity. But it was really only a prelude to the main event, which was the sappy stuff that was staged afterwards, with Leafs ancient and fresh.

Maple Leaf players line up along the blueline before their final game at Maple Leaf Gardens. (Bernard Weil/Toronto Star)

Asked if he was moved to tears by the evening, Gilmour snorted: "No, I don't cry."

The current Leafs—just showered and wearing their jerseys over their civvies—sat like well-behaved choir boys, so sweet, alongside coach Pat Quinn (Tie Domi with son Max on his lap) as upwards of a hundred Leaf predecessors, from the '30s through the '90s were introduced and applauded, as the 48th Highlanders softly played "The Maple Leaf Forever."

The loudest ovations were sometimes startling (Brian Glennie), more often predictable (Lanny McDonald, Borje Salming and Darryl Sittler).

How unfortunate that a few of the most distinguished in the Leaf panoply could either not attend (Wendel Clark, in action with the Tampa Bay Lightning) or chose to give these celebrations a pass (Dave Keon).

Fitting and fortunate, though, that former Leaf captain Doug Gilmour was right in the building, having just notched a goal and an assist against his ex-club, in a Chicago uniform.

Asked if he was moved to tears by the evening, Gilmour snorted: "No, I don't cry."

Which isn't true, because I saw him weep in the spring of '93, the spring of '94, the spring of '95...

The Gardens isn't dying. But it is being blanched, drained of its very lifeblood, with the Leafs relocating to the virgin Air Canada Centre, which can best be described as the Un-Gardens.

Despite all the other events held in MLG—the concerts and the conventions, the rodeos and the circuses, the evangelical meetings and the wrestling matches—this place is about hockey, it's about the Toronto Maple Leafs.

Not just the game itself, but the entirety of the experience: The parking crush and the College St. subway station and the heavy current of fans walking briskly towards the Gardens and the scalpers curbside and the smell of roasting chestnuts and pretty girls in their hockey sweaters and pimply boys in their team jackets and the clanging of the streetcar and horns tooting and...and...all of it.

These sensations, shared over the decades with friends and strangers, will not be so easily transferred to the Air Canada Centre at the stubby foot of Bay St. That's why Leaf president Ken Dryden, with all due respect, is wrong when he talks so eloquently about a moveable feast of memories.

It's not all in our heads. A lot of it was right here too, in this eclipsed building, on a Saturday night, with the Leafs on the ice.

That's why the organizers of last night's farewell pageant tapped into the well of nostalgia, by playing

These sensations, shared over the decades with friends and strangers, will not be so easily transferred to the Air Canada Centre at the stubby foot of Bay St.

jitterbug and big band music throughout the game; it's why some reporters up in the press box showed up wearing fedoras.

It's why a couple of opposing veterans from that original game at the Gardens—Toronto's Red Horner and Chicago's Harold "Mush" March, the latter the man who scored the first goal ever in this building—were brought together at centre ice for the ceremonial opening faceoff, using that very first-goal puck. But, at the end of an emotional week that has been larded with nostalgic musings, with oral history and written history and broadcast history, even I have to admit that...it was time. Enough.

The stories had all been told, every superannuated alumni interviewed, all the chapters of the Gardens Chronicles revisited.

Really, Maple Leaf Gardens—constructed by Conn Smythe in the depths of the Depression—was never intended for such bathos as this. It's too proud a building to suffer the slings of cheap sentimentality, however well-intentioned.

Yes, there were tears last night. And they were honestly shed. But the end has come and now, mercifully, fully, gone.

As someone who was falling out of love with me once said: "How can I miss you if you won't go away?" ●

Early Success and Then Despair

The Maple Leafs settle into their new digs at the Air Canada Centre and, under the steady guidance of coach Pat Quinn, qualify for the playoffs in the next five seasons. But then a new nine-year drought begins.

FAST FACTS

- Tie Domi is suspended for the remainder of the 2001 playoffs and the first eight games of the following season after his vicious elbow to the head of New Jersey defenceman Scott Niedermeyer.

- The Leafs sign goaltender Ed Belfour in July 2002. "The Eagle" plays in 170 over the next three seasons, posting a 93-61-15 record and recording 17 shutouts.

- The front office is revamped in 2003 when Larry Tanenbaum takes over from Steve Stavro as president of the organization. Ken Dryden leaves and John Ferguson, Jr. is hired as general manager.

- Paul Maurice takes over as head coach in 2006 and then gives way to Ron Wilson in 2008.

- In what is regarded as one of the worst deals in their history, the Leafs send draft pick goaltender Tuukku Rask to Boston for netminder Andrew Raycraft in June 2006. Rask goes on to win six individual awards (most valuable player in the NHL twice) and the Stanley Cup in 2011 and is still the Bruins' No. 1 goalie. Raycroft plays well in his first season in Toronto but is released in June 2008.

- Matt Sundin becomes a free agent in July 2008 after 13 seasons with the Leafs. He leaves with team career records for goals (420), points (987), game winning goals (79) and power-play goals (124). He signs with Vancouver in November, then retires at the end of the season.

- Peter Zezel, who played four seasons with the Leafs and had 608 points in 873 NHL games, dies of a rare blood disorder in May, 2009. He was 44.

- The Leafs take forward Nazem Kadri seventh over-all in the 2009 amateur draft, defenceman Morgan Rielly fifth over-all in 2012, forward Frederik Gauthier 21st in 2013 and forward William Nylander eighth in 2014. All are seen as key building blocks for the future.

- Richard Peddie, who was put in charge when the Leafs and the Raptors came together in 1998, steps down on December 31, 2011 after 14 years at the helm. He is succeeded by Tim Leiweke who gives way to Michael Friisdahl in October, 2015

- Randy Carlyle is hired as the team's head coach in March 2012, replacing Ron Wilson. He compiles a 91-78-19 record over four seasons then is axed in January 2015.

- The Leafs miss the playoffs for seven seasons beginning in the spring of 2006 before bowing out to Boston in the conference quarter-final in April, 2013.

Mats Sundin set Leafs team records for goals, points, game winning goals and powerplay goals.
(Tara Walton/Toronto Star)

Leafs Triumph in ACC Debut

First Puck Drops in Flashy New Era of Toronto Hockey

By Rosie DiManno • Published: February 21, 1999

From melancholia to merriment.

It doesn't take much to turn around a hockey crowd.

An overtime victory at the new Air Canada Centre, Toronto Maple Leafs 3-2 over the Montreal Canadiens, and poof! Old Maple Leaf Gardens was nothing more than a receding memory.

A week ago, there were tears and mournful goodbyes, at the ancient arena up at Church and Carlton. Last night, down on the foot of Bay, the wistfulness abruptly dissipated.

Todd Warriner scored the opening goal. Steve Thomas scored the closing goal. And now the Leafs are 1-and-0 in their new digs.

What's not to like?

The roof doesn't leak—which is more than can be said of the SkyDome on opening night.

The washrooms are grandiose—for those who find it necessary to watch TV while answering the call of nature.

The standing room area at the west end features a bar and an elbow ledge upon which to rest a glass of beer—but no smoking is permitted. For that luxury, one would have to be a member of the well-heeled Platinum Club where, in exchange for a whole lot of cabbage, the aristocratic (and corporate) classes can puff on cigars to their brass hearts' content, while also being allowed to stare from behind a braided rope at the players (the athletic specimens) as they stomp on and off the ice between periods.

Oh look Muffin, Mats Sundin has grown a goatee.

The Air Canada Centre is no rinky-dink rink, I admit.

But one could also very well wonder about the wisdom behind those same platinum seat suites, tucked windowless and unseeing beneath the bowels of the lower bowl: At least half the 18,800 customers last night seemed in no hurry to return for the action post-intermission, perhaps luxuriating in their poncy little warrens.

That left a great big chunk of empty seats, albeit comfy empty seats, vacant, giving the illusion—on television—that the new ACC draws as feeble a crowd as some of those latter-day monolithic arenas in the United States.

Terrific. A hockey rink where the fans prefer to watch the game on TV. How very 1999.

"I don't know where the people were," a befuddled Thomas said afterwards. "Maybe they were all downstairs having a beer. That took a little bit away from the atmosphere.

"Hey, if I was a fan, I'd probably be down there too."

But Thomas, to his credit, was not altogether without a sense of loss, for the Gardens. Motioning to his chest, he said: "I love this building. But the old building is still right here in my heart."

Well, at least there was a game on TV. And let us not belabour the point, no pun intended, that in order to ensure a coast-to-coast broadcast of this special game on Night One of this new era of hockey, the tall foreheads had to engage in a little deception.

The Leafs and the Canadiens line up for the opening faceoff at the Air Canada Centre. (David Cooper/Toronto Star)

That CBC technicians' strike cut the knees out from under the national broadcaster. But, as had been possibly long planned, CBC picked up the feed from ESPN2, and piped in the familiar voices of Bob Cole and Harry Neale, doing the play-by-play from a bomb shelter in Washington, or something.

This, one assumes, was preferable to inflicting the French-language broadcast on fans in Wawa and Lloydminster and Prince Rupert and places like that, where folks might not know a rondelle from a Rotorooter.

But here's the thing: The Air Canada Centre, much to my surprise, is not halfway hideous.

Once you're inside the building, anyway.

It provides all those amenities we apparently can't do without, although we were doing without quite nicely for the past 68 year at you-know-where.

Commodious corridors, spacious bathrooms, a multitude of concession outlets, great old framed photographs on the walls (many of these must have been kept in storage at the Gardens), a perky staff, those new powder blue uniforms for the usherettes,

a concerted effort at capturing the nostalgia of the just-vacated Maple Leaf Gardens.

And, if much of that nostalgia feels contrived, within the confines of the ACC, how many out there will truly complain? Nothing to be done about it now, anyhow.

True hockey fans care, first and foremostly, about the game. And the sight lines are fine. Or at least they're fine apart from those 129 seats that have been blocked off, shrouded in purple and green canvas, because one can see absolutely nothing from those particular vantage points.

Administrative staff were unable to tell us last night just how much revenue Steve Stavro et al are losing from the uselessness of those seats—which do, however, meet the minimum requirements for basket-ball. This was, after all, originally—before it became a hybrid facility—a basketball building, even if the poor Toronto Raptors (who debut there today) have been muscled aside.

An educated estimate, however, would put that lost revenue in the vicinity of a journeyman's hockey salary.

Steve Thomas and Sylvain Cote celebrated after Thomas scored the overtime winner in the first game at the Air Canada Centre. (Michael Stuparyk/Toronto Star)

I did think, though, that this structure was supposed to promote MORE NOISE, a less sedate atmosphere. Perhaps that will still prove to be the case, once a less dignified audience fills the house. Last night was corporate night, company night. If you had a company ticket, this was the one evening you'd make sure to use it. Just to be seen, if not necessarily to see.

No doubt, for games to come, many of those tickets will be passed on to more deserving, less anal-retentive types. Although the likelihood of an ordinary mook taking his kid to a Leaf game at the ACC is still remote.

There were nice touches, quite apart from the hockey game itself, which seemed, oddly, to lack the usual emotion of a Toronto-Montreal match-up, or maybe I was just too far removed, in the after-thought hockey press box, the Foster Hewitt Media Gondola, way, way, way up below the rafters.

"The bottom line is we won a hard game," said coach Pat Quinn, who noted also that the quality of the ice was poor and the players were unaccustomed to such bright lighting in the stands.

"That was a hard game all night long. It wasn't pretty, but it was a win."

Kurt Browning doing I'm not sure what in that pre-game ceremony—and, at least from the look of it, doing it on hockey skates instead of figure skating blades—was unexpected, and not without a certain charm, particularly with the addition of all those munchkin hockey players doing line-dancing type drills.

It felt more light-hearted, less larded by the heavy hand of memory and melancholy, than did those overly-panned closing ceremony events from a week earlier.

The banners unfurling were appropriately dramatic, although not as high-tech as many spectators probably realized. From that new catwalk, high above centre ice, behind-the-scenes employees released the rolled up gonfalons in almost perfect unison with the zinging fireworks and sound effects.

They're not, obviously, the same banners that hung from the roof at the Gardens. They're certainly not the banners that were transported from the Gardens during Friday's cutesy-sweet moving-out parade. But they were pretty cool, and a reminder of former glory, no matter how long-past.

Not just the 11 Stanley Cup banners, but the blue-tinted depictions of honoured players and those (two) whose numbers have actually been retired: Bill Barilko (5) and Ace Bailey (6), along with Syl Apps (he died, alas, just this past Christmas), Charlie Conacher, King Clancy, Turk Broda, Johnny Bower, Tim Horton, Teeder Kennedy, George Armstrong.

A couple of those fellows were in the house last night, in a corporeal sense. One likes to believe that, spiritually, the rest of them were present, too.

The high-definition video board, a long-belated and long-deferred feature which regular Leaf-goers had been denied at the Gardens, was busy with the usual offering of promos and advertisements and yadda yadda yadda. Few of those in attendance seemed particularly captivated by it. The instant replays were appreciated but we'd become accustomed to doing without.

There were notable glitches, too: The radar-gun that was measuring the speed of slapshots taken by contestants during the second intermission didn't work. A pizza oven on the second level went on the fritz. Some other cooking equipment faltered.

"Anytime you open a building for the first time, you'll have some problems," said building manager Bob Hunter. "We fired all the equipment and tested it and cooked with it. But what can you do? Tomorrow's a whole new ballgame."

Wrong sport, mister.

Unfortunate, however, that in this entire new design there was no place for the one fan-oriented feature at the Gardens for which the public could truly thank Steve Stavro, because it had been his idea: The glass-paned doors at the south end, up there on Carlton St., where passersby could drop in and peek through, if only for a fleeting glimpse of a game or a practice.

President/GM Ken Dryden is on record as saying that was a detail that most impressed him when he returned to the Gardens in his executive capacity. But no such porthole of access exists at the Air Canada Centre.

"Yes, that's too bad," said Dryden, with what sounded like genuine regret. "There was just no way to incorporate that into the design.

"But...maybe...later on, we can try to bring that back. At some point in the future."

There's nothing but future, here. ●

Colour Burke Black 'n Blue

New GM Promises More 'Truculence and Belligerence'

By Paul Hunter • Published: November 30, 2008

No more Mr. Nice Guys—the blue and white are about to get a little more black and blue.

Brian Burke, after being introduced as the 13th general manager of the Maple Leafs, promised that his team—and it is very much that now—will evolve into a pull-no-punches, in-your-face squad, an approach reflective of the guy now calling the shots.

"We require, as a team, proper levels of pugnacity, testosterone, truculence and belligerence. That's how our teams play," said Burke.

"I make no apologies for that. Our teams play a North American game. We're throwbacks. It's black-and-blue hockey. It's going to be more physical hockey here than people are used to."

Burke said he believes in very aggressive pursuit of the puck and physical contact in all three zones. To help achieve that, he also wants the Maple Leafs to get bigger.

"We'll see if we can address that internally, if (recent call-up Andre) Deveaux is the answer or we have another internal answer or if we have to go get it. The first thing and probably the easiest thing to change on your team is the amount of the snarl, the amount of the bite. That's an important part of how my teams play," he said.

Burke won a Stanley Cup in Anaheim with a team that hit first, asked questions later and relished fisticuffs. That Ducks team led the league in fights and penalty minutes and had only two European skaters that were regulars in the lineup.

Beyond the fact that the 53-year-old said he likes that type of hockey, Burke said it helps create a safer, cocoon-like environment for developing players, something the Leafs will have a lot of over the next few years.

"That's how you provide a fear-free environment for your young players. That's how you develop young players where they don't have to worry about picking their teeth out of the glass or getting their faces washed," he said.

Head coach Ron Wilson is on board but said it takes time to change a team's approach.

"The bigger the better, the faster the better, the more physical the better," he said. "But you have to have patience. Just because we hired Brian today doesn't mean we're going to (immediately) play like the Philadelphia Flyers from 1975. We just don't have that right now."

Burke's love of physical hockey has been interpreted as a disdain for European players and the Leafs have 10 of them, including goaltender Vesa Toskala, on their current roster.

But the new GM said that assessment is completely false and he pointed to Niklas Hagman, a Finn, and Mikhail Grabovski, a German-born Belarussian, as two players from the current squad who have impressed him.

"I don't care where players are born. I don't care where they come from. I don't care what colour their passport is. But they've either got to be a contributing offensive player in our top six forwards or they've got to be a hard-hat guy in our bottom six," he said. "If they can't fill a role, regardless of what their passport says, then they're not going to be here."

Burke has a contract for the rest of this season and another five years at approximately $18 million (U.S.) in total.

In addition to being the general manager he is also the Leafs' president.

Burke was blunt and to the point in his first day on the job, noting that he phoned Raptors president and GM Bryan Colangelo before signing on just to make sure his basketball counterpart did indeed have the necessary autonomy to do his job.

"He said, 'Yes.' That's good enough for me," said Burke.

He will be asking Anaheim for permission to interview Dave Nonis, who works there as a senior adviser in hockey operations.

Nonis is expected to join Burke in Toronto soon as the assistant GM.

He likely won't be reshaping the team immediately because he has a self-imposed trade freeze of Dec. 9—10 days ahead of the NHL's—because he believes players should be able to spend the holidays uninterrupted with their families.

He doesn't believe in no-trade contracts, a clause in five Leaf contracts last spring that severely handcuffed the team at the trade deadline.

"I've given one no-trade clause in my life and it was for medical reasons to J.S. Giguere. His son had a medical condition that required him going to UCLA medical hospital for years. Other than that, I don't like them. I think they're coach killers."

While outgoing GM Cliff Fletcher has a job for "as long as he wants one, "the rest of the front office will have to prove itself, much like his players. ●

Brian Burke wanted Leafs to play with a combination of "pugnacity, testosterone, truculence and belligerence."
(Richard Lautens/Toronto Star)

Leafs Snag Sniper in Kessel

Burke Surrenders Three Picks for Speedy Winger

By Paul Hunter • Published: September 19, 2009

The future has arrived for the Maple Leafs.

In a trade that accelerates Toronto's building process dramatically, the Leafs acquired star winger Phil Kessel, a 36-goal scorer who should provide the club with some much-needed offence and develop as a building block with some of the other young talent Toronto has already assembled.

The Leafs did pay "a steep price" for Kessel, as general manager Brian Burke acknowledged, sending Boston two first-round draft picks—one in 2010, the other in 2011—and a second-round pick in 2010.

But Kessel won't turn 22 until Oct. 2 and Burke said he felt comfortable moving the picks because the Leafs have other young players, such as college grads Tyler Bozak, Christian Hanson, Viktor Stalberg and this year's top pick, Nazem Kadri, and free agents Jonas Gustavsson and Robert Slaney, that the team has acquired through free agency or the draft.

"We feel by stocking the cupboard, we can take some of the cans off the shelf for the future," said Burke. "It's a statement to our players that we intend to be competitive right away."

Kessel agreed to a five-year, $27 million contract. His cap hit will be $5.4 million a season, something the Leafs can accommodate.

Leaf winger Jason Blake, who has spent some time with Kessel in the past, was excited to see a player of his ability join the team.

"I know we're in a rebuilding process right now, but it just shows the commitment, that we want to put a winning team on the ice," he said.

"He's just another piece of the puzzle, but he's a tremendous player. I know him a little bit, being an American, and he's a good team guy and he'll definitely boost our hockey club. The offence he brings definitely makes our team a lot better."

There have been questions about Kessel's personality in the past and suggestions that he is a corrosive dressing room presence, often distant from his teammates and too much of a "me" guy in a game in which even the stars put team aspirations first.

But Burke said the winger has been largely misunderstood because of his shyness. The GM said he is completely

Phil Kessel led the Maple Leafs in scoring for six seasons after being obtained in a trade with Boston. (Rene Johnston/Toronto Star)

"It's a statement to our players that we intend to be competitive right away."

comfortable dealing for Kessel after spending time with the native of Madison, Wisc., on the national level in the past.

Burke is also the general manager of the American Olympic team and was reassured by Kessel's behaviour at that team's summer camp.

"I'll tell you a story," said Burke, harkening back to an American camp in Portland, Me., before last year's world championship when a fishing trip was planned as a team outing. "The captain, Jeff Halpern, asked Phil if he wanted to go. Phil said, 'I get seasick in a bathtub. I have trouble even fishing on a lake.'

"So Halpern said, 'I guess that's a no.' But Phil said, 'If the guys are going, I'm going.' He went, puked his guts out but did it because it was a team function.

"People remember his draft year, he was a real shy person. But he's really come into his own. He's more engaging and outgoing and his personality is showing through as he gets comfortable with life in the National Hockey League."

Although Kessel was a 60-point man for Boston, which had selected him fifth overall in the 2006 draft, he was a restricted free agent. He could not reach a deal with the Bruins, who were pushed up against the salary cap. When talks with Boston turned acrimonious, Kessel said he would not return.

That rejuvenated talks with the Leafs, who tried to land to Kessel on draft day in a deal that would have sent defenceman Tomas Kaberle and a pick to the Bruins. That fell apart due to miscommunication over which pick would be included, and Kaberle's no-trade clause kicked in again.

Kessel won't be able to play with the Leafs until he recovers from shoulder surgery, but is expected to return to game action in mid-November. He is skating but is not ready for contact or shooting.

"It'll be a while before our fans see him, but he'll bring tremendous foot speed. He should improve our power play and he's a good shootout player and in our game, that's an important asset," said Burke. "He's a dynamic player." Though Burke has been working on getting Kessel for some time, he said he felt even more comfortable trading the picks after seeing how solid some of his prospects have looked early in camp.

"They've justified our faith in them," he said.

Coach Ron Wilson said he could see Kessel some-day skating on a line with a play-making centre such as Kadri or Bozak when those youngsters are regulars.

The Leafs are obviously confident that Kessel will continue to mature as a top-level scorer. He had 11 goals as a rookie and bumped that to 19 in his sophomore campaign. His breakout campaign came last year when he skated alongside centre Marc Savard.

Kessel was diagnosed with testicular cancer in 2006. Following surgery, Kessel returned to the Bruins' lineup and won the Masterton Trophy for dedication to hockey. ●

Sudden Impact!

Burke Pulls Trigger on Deals for Phaneuf and Giguere

By Damien Cox • Published: February 1, 2010

In theory, it should have been the dreadful Maple Leafs panicking and being forced to shed a potential all-star player for immediate help or, at the very least, immediate change for the sake of change.

This is a franchise, after all, that is historically well versed in the dark arts of blind, illogical panic.

But in the case of Sunday's deal between the Leafs and the Calgary Flames that brings flashy, hard-hitting Dion Phaneuf east, it's possible, but unlikely, Toronto fans will ever regret this trade in the same way some whine and moan on a daily basis over the first-round draft picks sacrificed to acquire scoring winger Phil Kessel.

Calgary fans, on the other hand, may one day view Jan.31, 2010 in the same painful way they still lament Jan.2, 1992, the day Doug Gilmour went to the Leafs in a massive 10-player trade.

That's not to say Phaneuf is a lock to be a star at the Air Canada Centre. The very fact that he was made available tells you that the Flames, at least, view Phaneuf as a flawed young defenceman with questionable hockey sense, one unlikely to approach the form that made him a 2008 Norris Trophy finalist.

The fact he has a monstrous contract for a relatively unproven 24-year-old blueliner—four years left on a six-year deal with $25.5 million (all figures U.S.) still owed—just

made his shortcomings seem more yawning, in the same way Bryan McCabe seemed worse as a Leaf than he actually was because of his pay cheque.

But Calgary GM Darryl Sutter was also in a deteriorating position, and if his trading partner, Leaf hockey boss Brian Burke, ends up smelling like roses on this deal, it will be because of a confluence of factors that rushed Sutter into a deal he might not otherwise have wanted to make.

For starters, Phaneuf and his Calgary teammate, Robyn Regehr, apparently didn't get along. Regehr, according to some, viewed Phaneuf as arrogant and unwilling to listen. Phaneuf found Regehr equally unbearable to work with because Regehr was always trying to offer instructions and directions.

The Leafs were aware of this. Just guessing, but Wayne Primeau, a former Flame, might have confirmed their suspicions.

Sutter's team also has severe offensive shortcomings, something that wasn't addressed convincingly by the acquisition of Olli Jokinen from Phoenix last March. The Flames needed to find some goals, not so easy in the NHL where a 36-goal scorer like Kessel, for example, had cost a heavy price.

Finally, the Flames had started to lose, and lose a lot. Prior to Saturday's win over awful Edmonton, the Flames had shockingly

another young, mistake-prone defenceman prematurely dumped by a team striving for a championship that could no longer stomach the errors. Then again, he could be McCabe. Oodles of tools, not enough toolbox.

Phaneuf, Kessel and Luke Schenn are now the future for the Leafs, along with Jonas Gustavsson—now to be mentored by newly arrived J.S. Giguere—Nazem Kadri, Tyler Bozak, Viktor Stalberg and Christian Hanson, likely to be recalled to the parent club Monday. Maybe even lanky Keith Aulie can be part of a future Leaf defence corps.

If Giguere, available all season and urgently so after Jonas Hiller signed an $18 million deal last week, can solidify the Leaf crease even a little bit, a blue line of Mike Komisarek, Tomas Kaberle, Francois Beauchemin, Schenn and Phaneuf may start to look formidable.

Given where the Leafs are in the standings—29th out of 30 teams—it's somewhat extraordinary they could make a deal like they did to acquire Phaneuf.

lost nine straight, scoring a total of 14 goals in those defeats.

Leaf fans, soured by the season, had reason to no longer be enamoured of Matt Stajan, Niklas Hagman and Ian White. But to the Flames, that troika represented a quick infusion of offence and a convenient solution to a dressing room problem.

But the cost was startling. Phaneuf could prove to be something we've seen many times in NHL history,

This swap was the product of a showdown between two experienced, battled-hardened GMs. Maybe Sutter knows something Burke doesn't. Or maybe Burke, in a lousy bargaining position, identified a pressure point with another team and used it to grab a raw jewel in the kind of exciting, multi-player hockey trade thought to have vanished with the red line. ●

Defenceman Dion Phaneuf was the centrepiece in a seven-player deal that sent Niklas Hagman, Matt Stajan, Jamal Mayers and defenceman Ian White to Calgary. (Steve Russell/Toronto Star)

Heartbroken Nation

Leafs Blow Three-Goal Lead in Game 7 before Falling in Overtime to Bruins

By Damien Cox • Published: May 14, 2013

Defeat, in the end, came with abrupt finality, with a sense of shock and surprise and even momentary disbelief that what seemed to be the start of something special was over.

What, no more games? That's it?

Oh my word. They lost it how?

The Maple Leafs, and their legions of fans, had dared to dream that this might become a unique spring, particularly after twice fighting off elimination to force Game 7 in their best-of-seven opening round playoff series against the favoured Boston Bruins.

All signs were pointing to this series as a shiny new beginning, not a nightmarish end.

Instead, the end came with a stunning, mind-blowing 5-4 overtime loss on Monday night, with defeat snatched from the jaws of victory in the most painful, shocking and unforgettable way imaginable.

A commanding two-goal lead with less than 90 seconds to play.

Choked away.

There will be explanations, and excuses, and scapegoats. Fingers will be pointed. A season that seemed a joyous surprise turned, in a matter of minutes, into a Leaf horror show.

Sure, they were huge underdogs going into this series, and yes, this was a season in which few picked them even to make the playoffs. Still, it will take a long, long time for Leaf fans to forget this one. The hockey world will reference this complete and utter collapse for years to come.

In a game totally abandoned by the officials to the nastiest desires of two of the NHL's toughest teams, the visitors led 4-1 with less than 11 minutes left in the third period and seemed headed to the second round with a stunning upset victory.

No team in the modern tight-checking NHL blows a lead like that, right?

Well, the Leafs did in what will live on as one of the more infamous playoff defeats in team history, with Patrice Bergeron's OT winner completing one of the most extraordinary Game 7 comebacks in NHL history.

Until it ended, it seemed everything was breaking the Leafs' way. They'd won the previous two games, holding the B's to one goal in each, then had been able to

fly to Boston on Sunday night after Game 6 while the Bruins were stranded in Toronto, unable to fly home because of a plane malfunction.

The stars were aligning. Chief operating officer Tom Anselmi arrived with his lucky tie. Boston was hurting badly on the blue line, down to just a handful of healthy bodies, seemingly too beaten up to fight on.

And then the Bruins, with the hearts of champions, demonstrated the stars were aligning for them, not the Leafs.

The Leafs carried a 2-1 lead into the third period, then seemed to break the game open with two more goals in the opening six minutes of the third. First, Phil Kessel banged in his fourth goal of the series. The fact the sequence began with Kessel muscling big Milan Lucic off the puck in the Boston end seemed to signal the home team had run out of fight.

Kessel then assisted on a goal by Nazem Kadri off a 2-on-1 break just 3:20 later to give the Leafs their first three-goal lead of the series.

Over, it seemed.

But the Bruins, Cup winners in 2011, weren't done.

First Nathan Horton made it 4-2, then with the goalie pulled for an extra attacker, Lucic made it 4-3 with just 1:22 to go. And 31 seconds after that, with the Leafs desperately hanging on and the Boston net empty again, Bergeron wristed a high shot from the blue line through a Zdeno Chara screen to, unbelievably, tie the game.

Two goals in 31 seconds. Incredible.

When OT arrived, a bitter conclusion for the Leafs seemed inevitable even after Joffrey Lupul blasted a shot that Tuukka Rask needed to make a fabulous save on to keep the game tied.

Finally, Bergeron delivered the dagger at 6:05 of the extra session on a play where three Leafs - Cody Franson, Jake Gardiner and Mikhail Grabovski—all had a chance to make an easy clear. But could not.

This, folks, is the kind of defeat that can scar a team. After nine years out of the playoffs, the Leafs were finally back in the post-season tournament and on the verge of winning a round against big odds. They'll have to analyze exactly how they blew it, which players didn't measure up when history—the Leafs hadn't come back from a 3-1 playoff deficit since 1942—came knocking.

You don't just shrug off defeats like this. Just as it seemed the Leafs had answered important questions about goaltending and team leadership, it all collapsed in an ugly, smoking heap.

It was right there, easily in hand. And then, in a matter of moments, it wasn't, and the Leafs joined Montreal and Vancouver on the sidelines as the chase for the Cup by seven U.S. squads and the Ottawa Senators continues.

The end came for the Leafs in a way few who follow this seemingly star-crossed franchise will soon forget. ●

Brad Marchand's overtime goal in Game 7 completed Boston's Game 7 comeback and sent the Leafs to a crushing defeat. (Steve Russell/Toronto Star)

Back to the Drawing Board

Hiring of Brendan Shanahan signals a complete change of direction as Burke, Nonis and Carlyle are out and Babcock and Lamoriello are in. Toronto fans are promised pain before success and the Leafs deliver—in spades.

FAST FACTS

- Former coach Pat Burns is inducted into the Hockey Hall of Fame in June 2014—four years after losing his long battle with cancer. He was 58 at the time of his death.

- The Leafs finish in 27th place in April 2015 and President Brendan Shanahan fires GM Dave Nonis, coach Peter Horachek and three of his assistants the day after the season ends.

- The Leafs use the fourth over-all pick in the 2015 amateur draft to grab skilled forward Mitch Marner. Marner has a standout 2015-16 season with his junior club, the London Knights, as they capture the Memorial Cup.

- The real makeover (and the real pain for Leafs fans) begins on July 1, 2015 when leading scorer Phil Kessel is dealt to Pittsburgh for Kasperi Kapanen, Scott Harrington and Nick Spaling.

- Lou Lamoriello steps down as president of the New Jersey Devils in late July 2015 to become the Leafs' 16th general manager. He joins a beefed up front office that includes assistant GM Kyle Dubas and director of player personnel Mark Hunter.

- Former captain Dave Keon, goalie Turk Broda and defenceman Tim Horton are inducted into Legends Row on January 21, 2016. Their statues join those of Johnny Bower, Darryl Sittler, Borje Salming, Mats Sundin, Ted Kennedy, George Armstrong and Syl Apps in Toronto's Maple Leaf Square.

- GM Lou Lamoriello announces on April 16, 2016 that the team has signed centre Nazem Kadri and defenceman Morgan Rielly to six-year contract extensions.

- John Brophy, who coached the Leafs for more than two seasons during the tumultuous 1980s, dies at a nursing home in his hometown of Antigonish, N.S. on May 23, 2016. He was 83.

- The Leafs deal a couple of draft picks to the Anahein Ducks on June 20, 1916 in exchange for goaltender Frederik Anderson and promptly sign him to a five-year, $25-million contract. Three weeks later, erstwhile No. 1 goalie Jonathan Bernier is sent packing to the Ducks for a conditional 2017 draft pick.

Nazem Kadri was signed to a six-year contract extension in April 2016. (Lucas Oleniuk/Toronto Star)

Fear, Pain and a Long Journey

Mike Babcock Knows What He's Getting into with Leafs

By Bruce Arthur • Published: May 22, 2015

On Tuesday night, Mike Babcock had a plan, and in the middle of the night it changed. His daughter was printing her last high school paper at 3:32 a.m., and it woke him up, and by morning there was a new plan. Many sage people in hockey believed very firmly that Mike Babcock was never coming to this fevered city, for good and solid reasons. He won't say what tipped the balance, but on Thursday he was here, saying he didn't come here just to make the playoffs.

"As a coach, you are in the day-to-day winning business, and you understand," said Babcock, who signed an eight-year, $50-million (US) deal.

"I have been in it a long time. On game day I will be shortsighted for sure. But I have a big picture in mind, so does Shanny, so does Larry, so do the people on our staff and that is where we are going.

"But if you think there is no pain coming, there is pain coming."

Brendan Shanahan was so honest about that in their first meeting that he worried he'd blown it, and Babcock says he understood.

For all the worries about whether he could be patient, early on Babcock asked Maple Leaf Sports & Entertainment minority owner Larry Tanenbaum, "Are you willing to stick with it when its hard, when it's really hard, are you going to be in, for sure?" He knew how bad it was, here.

So why did Babcock come? If he was going to be rich, why not go to Buffalo, home of some bluer-chip talent and a comparable offer, and some of whose reporters barked pointed questions to Babcock about the Sabres believing they had a deal? (The rivalry could be fun again, very soon.)

Babcock cited the challenge, his family, the smarts of the front office. (Of director of player personnel Mark Hunter, Babcock was effusive, saying "I can talk to that guy. He's a hockey man.")

He cited the opportunity to become empty nesters in a downtown condo with his wife Maureen.

He cited the Leafs history, which is nice.

The only part that truly impresses people is the generational devotion, and that can be claustrophobic, but sure.

The tipping point itself, however, remains a mystery. It's a bigger and better city than Buffalo, with a deeper tradition. Maybe it was as simple as that.

Still, it's going to take years here, if the payoff happens at all, and Babcock is emphatically not wired to lose. Asked about the occasion in his coaching career when he's faced the most sustained challenges, Babcock mentioned Spokane, where he had one bad year on two different occasions, 20 years ago. He's missed the playoffs once in the NHL. Not coincidentally, Babcock talked about the positive effects of fear.

"Fear is a great thing," said Babcock. "In 1997 I was bear hunting and I got the call and they said you were going to coach the world junior team. And right away I thought, 'Oh my god, they just won four or five in a row, what am I getting myself into?' When Steve Yzerman had me in his office and said Mike, you are coaching the 2010 Olympic

team, when I got to my truck I was scared to death. What did I get myself into? Same thing in 2014.

"I meant that was exhilarating. It is about being alive. I'm 52. I'm not ready to die. I want to get on with it. It is about the journey, it is about trying to maximize your potential and squeeze every ounce out of yourself. When I talked to Shanny, that is what I heard."

Babcock was full of plainspoken aphorisms and said the right things, and this city will love him, to start. There have been so many weddings at the Air Canada Centre, grand ceremonies, a public taking of vows. Brian Burke's is the one we all remember, but there have been more: Tim Leiweke, Brendan Shanahan, Masai Ujiri, on and on. This town is never short of saviours, and somehow has yet to be saved.

"He's a guy that you can count on," said Tanenbaum. "Ours is a long-term plan. Ours is not a plan to come in here and make a dramatic change and leave, OK? And that's why we were talking eight years, 10 years." Asked why it was different than, say, Burke, Tanenbaum had an answer.

"You have seen some weddings here, there's no question about it. When you look at Brian Burke—and I love Brian, he's a great, great guy—but Brian wanted to be the show. What Brian wanted to be was his hands on the steering wheel, nobody else's. If there was a Shanny here, he didn't want a Shanny. If there was a Mike Babcock, he didn't want Mike Babcock. So you put 100% of your faith in Brian Burke.

"In this case, we're looking at building a team here. And that team is Mark Hunter, it's Kyle Dubas, it's Brendan Shanahan, it's Mike Babcock. Because nobody's got the answers for everything."

More smart people is a hopeful thing, and now we'll see if it holds together, and bears fruit. Scotty Bowman won four straight Stanley Cups in Montreal and spent seven frustrating years in Buffalo before leaving to find something better. Mike Babcock had an agonizing time making this decision, and he made it at the last minute, knowing everything he knew. But that part is over. He's committed to eight years, no outs, and pain. Whatever Mike Babcock felt about this place before, he's a Leaf, and there's no turning back now. ●

Mike Babcock decided at the last-minute to accept the offer to coach the Maple Leafs. (Cole Burston/Toronto Star)

Leafs Give Sundin a Spot on Legends Row

'As a Player, You Never Have Time to Take It All In'

By Mark Zwolinski • Published: August 15, 2009

Mats Sundin once said he would never trade his 13 seasons as a Maple Leaf for a Stanley Cup ring. It was that commitment to the blue and white – a weave of dedication and consistency—that made him one of the most beloved Leafs captains, and something the Leafs have immortalized on the team's Legends Row.

The popular Swede's inclusion in the Row was announced Thursday evening when the Leafs opened their Fan Fest at the Air Canada Centre. Fans were expecting the addition of one player—Borje Salming—to the row, but a crowd of about 2,500 was taken by surprise when Leafs president Brendan Shanahan called out Sundin's name. Sundin was equally surprised when he was informed.

"I was shocked, you don't expect to be part of Legends Row and the names they have up there (so soon), " Sundin told the Fan Fest audience. "At my age now (44), I thought I'd get there down the road, so it's great to be there now.

"As a player you never have the time to take it all in...Now (I) have the time and I have a 3-year-old daughter with me, and a 10-month-old son, and I hope they bring their children back here one day and look at (the statue) too."

Sundin was especially proud to join Salming; he said Salming and Mats Naslund were players he idolized growing up.

Syl Apps and George Armstrong were previously announced as 2015 Legends Row inductees and their statues will be unveiled in November during the Hockey Hall of Fame induction weekend.

"It's kinda tough to describe what this means to me and my family...those are great names there, it's a real honour," Sundin said.

Shanahan broke the Legends Row news to Sundin earlier in the summer, and the Big Swede's reaction included disbelief and even an expletive.

"Mats and I bump into one another once in a while," Shanahan said. "We never played on the same team together, but we have a relationship. We met (at a downtown Toronto hotel) and he was pleased it happened so soon (after his playing career), and the fact he went in with Borje Salming."

Both Sundin and Salming had their likeness reproduced in bronze by Rockford, Ill., sculptor Erik Blome. The Leafs will hold an unveiling ceremony with both players on hand Saturday morning.

The bronze immortalization marks perhaps the final Leafs tribute to Sundin, though he still maintains a home in Toronto and is a frequent visitor to the hockey city he called his second home.

Sundin joked with reporters after addressing the Fan Fest crowd, saying he hoped his statue would have him wearing a CCM helmet and not the Jofa helmet he wore at the outset of his career.

Over his 13 seasons as a Leaf—11 of them as captain—he guided Toronto to six straight post-seasons between 1998 and 2004, before

winding up the Toronto era of his Hall of Fame career in 2008 as the club's all-time leading scorer.

Sundin scored at least 70 points in each of his 13 Leafs seasons, save for the lockout shortened 1994-95 season. He led the team in scoring every year in Toronto except for 2002-03, when Alex Mogilny topped him by seven points.

He left the Leafs as a free agent and retired after a season and a half with Vancouver, finishing with 1,349 points over 1,346 career games in the NHL.

He was also the first Swedish player to score 500 NHL goals.

Sundin has been watching the summer of change in Toronto, and likes what he sees.

"I think Brendan Shanahan and his team are doing the right thing, building the organization from the ground up," Sundin said.

"Leafs fans will have their Stanley Cup." ●

Mats Sundin greeted fans as he arrived for induction into Legends Row. (Cole Burston/Toronto Star)

Leafs' Rebuild Gaining Momentum

Shanahan Has Shown No Fear in Making Tough Decisions

By Damien Cox • Published: February 13, 2016

And, that's a wrap. On Episode One. Phase One. Chapter One. Whatever you'd like to call it.

The End of the Beginning?

With the trading of captain Dion Phaneuf this week, Brendan Shanahan and Co. effectively completed the opening stage of the most ambitious, aggressive rebuild in the long history of the Maple Leafs, one that has not yet moved the club closer to becoming a champion again one day but has emphatically ended a frustrating decade of drifting no closer to that goal.

From May 2004 to May 2015 there were two CEOs, four general managers, five different head coaches, 18 starting goalies, one major ownership change, three years when the club didn't draft in the first round, a period of investment in muscle when the rest of the league was going in the opposite direction and, lest we forget, one seven-game playoff defeat.

Phaneuf's departure, however, ended any uncertainty the Leafs really have embarked on a definitive new path. They've taken it down to the studs, intentionally getting much worse in the hopes of getting much better some day.

You may not agree with it, but there's absolutely no confusion about what they are doing. Those who doubted Shanahan would have the gumption and political capital to do what previous Leaf hockey executives said the Toronto hockey market would never accept have been proven wrong.

While not totally a clean slate — there's millions of dollars in "dead" money on the books and a few highly paid vets still around — the major subtracting can now end and the adding can truly begin.

The Leafs have no active players under contract past the conclusion of the 2017-18 season other than Jake Gardiner. That provides a handy reference point; every new contract now has to be signed within the context of whether that player fits in 2018 and beyond.

Now, it's the next stage that's really going to require brains, judgment and ingenuity.

That's Chapter Two — adding many more roster pieces that are viable and reflect a specific team identity and philosophy.

Chapter Three will then be about blending those players into a .500 team, and the chapter after that will be getting back to the post-season.

Chapter Five? Well, that's the one with the most pages, the one that may meander around indefinitely, perhaps never getting to the final thrilling conclusion, because the NHL is a very difficult, competitive pro league and there's no sure-fire way to get to the top.

Ask the Washington Capitals. They drafted superstar Alex Ovechkin 12 years ago and may, just may, have the team to finally win a Stanley Cup this spring.

So even if Mitch Marner is even somewhat Ovechkin-like in his offensive potential (his

They've taken it down to the studs, intentionally getting much worse in the hopes of getting much better some day.

biggest boosters suggest he's more like Patrick Kane) it's entirely conceivable that 11 years from now the Leafs may have diligently stuck to their plans, used possession-first hockey and enhanced sports science and hockey analytics effectively and yet may still be trying to find a way to get to a Cup final, let alone win it.

So if you're a fan and don't want to abandon all hope now, you don't look at Chapter Five. You leave your cynicism and bad memories at the door and focus on Chapter Two, which will almost certainly be a blast if you can ignore the win-loss column at least some of the time and enjoy the process of collecting young hockey players and charting their progress.

Start with 21-year-old defenceman Morgan Rielly, a developing talent already on the Leaf roster. Then there's William Nylander, just a step away at Ricoh Coliseum leading a very strong, very young Marlies team that is all about speed and skill, the new organizational mantra.

For former scoring star Phil Kessel, last year the Leafs received forward Kasperi Kapanen, who scored the gold-medal winning goal at this year's world junior championship. Along with Marner last June, they drafted defenceman Travis Dermott, winger Jeremy Bracco, defenceman Andrew Nielsen and forward Dmytro Timashov.

For Phaneuf, the Leafs picked up several pieces, including former Oshawa Generals winger Tobias Lindberg and a second-round pick in 2017. This spring, should Pittsburgh and Sidney Crosby make the post-season, Toronto will have two first round selections, their own likely in the top five (Auston Matthews, Jesse Puljujarvi, Matthew Tkachuk?) and perhaps another (from the Kessel deal) in the top 20.

They're set to sign 22-year-old KHL free agent Nikita Zaitsev, a defenceman, and will pursue Harvard senior forward Jimmy Vesey this summer if Nashville is unable to sign their former draft pick and he becomes a free agent.

Lots of names, lots of youthful promise. That's what makes Chapter Two enjoyable.

The last time the Leafs headed down this road was in the 1980s when they set out on a plan (of sorts) to emphasize youth and drafted Gary Nylund, Ken Wreggett, Wendel Clark, Russ Courtnall, Al Iafrate, Vince Damphousse, Gary Leeman, Todd Gill, Luke Richardson, Allan Bester and Scott Pearson. That was built on the destructive ownership of Harold Ballard and never amounted to much.

By contrast, in Shanahan, coach Mike Babcock, GM Lou Lamoriello and Mark Hunter, among others, the current club has established a stable infrastructure of experienced, talented people with championship resumes. Maple Leaf Sports and Entertainment has, by paying Babcock $50 million (U.S.) and absorbing various financial commitments (Nathan Horton) so they don't show up on the salary cap balance sheet, demonstrated a willingness to follow Shanahan's plan.

Not every prospect or draft pick will make it. Since September, the Leafs have dealt prospects Carter Verhaeghe, Tom Nilsson, Matt Finn, Chris Gibson, Ryan Rupert, Cody Donaghey and Casey Bailey.

There will be curves and swerves along the way and the trajectory may be maddening. Just ask Edmonton. Nobody really knows how long Lamoriello plans to be around. There will be attempts to accelerate the process, like possibly taking a run at Steven Stamkos this summer.

But this, Chapter Two, could be the most enjoyable part of the entire rebuild, the part that inspires imagination and possibilities before the rude competitive realities of the NHL interrupt.

This is the part where the team and its fans just get to dream. ●

One Giant Leap

Leafs Land Crown Jewel Matthews in NHL Draft

By Bruce Arthur • Published: June 25, 2016

Mats Sundin strolled the red carpet at the Hockey Hall of Fame in 2014, and he looked relaxed. Asked how he was doing, the retired captain of the Toronto Maple Leafs sighed and smiled. He was so happy, he said, now that the pressure was off. The pressure of playing for Sweden and, most of all, the pressure of playing for the Leafs. Sundin said it was easier to be captain when you're not from Ontario, but it was a heavy burden, regardless. He just looked so relieved.

On Friday night, one year after they missed Connor McDavid by a ping-pong ball, the Toronto Maple Leafs drafted centre Auston Matthews of Scottsdale, Ariz., No. 1 overall. Toronto had not selected No. 1 overall since Wendel Clark in 1985, but Sundin was one of those. Matthews is expected to be a franchise centre, and those are rare beasts.

"I mean, hockey's a team game, so there's really no saviour," Matthews said. "I want to be an impact player. I believe I can be a franchise centreman, a No. 1 centreman in the NHL, so that's my ultimate goal."

The Brendan Shanahan-led rebuild of this franchise has had many steps: the ejection of the previous regime, man by man; the front-office reconstruction; Mike Babcock and Lou Lamoriello. There are prospects all through the system now, at varying degrees of development: There is the makings of something.

And now, a crown jewel: a big centre who can handle the puck and eat tough minutes and who excelled against men as an 18-year-old. Auston Matthews, welcome to Toronto.

"My heart was beating when I was walking up there," Matthews said. "Very nerve-wracking."

"I remember somebody at the end-of-season press conference last year, after I said we're going to do this the right way, asking, 'Well what if you win the draft lottery?'" Leafs president Brendan Shanahan said. "Well, then it's going to speed up. So the answer is it's still a team game that requires a solid team. Acquiring special players helps."

Pressure. A No. 1 pick guarantees nothing, of course. Go back to Sundin in 1989, and four No. 1 picks have played central roles in winning Stanley Cups with the team that drafted them: Vincent Lecavalier, Marc-André Fleury and Sidney Crosby on the same team, Patrick Kane. That's it.

But when you have great players to build around, you have a chance to build something great. With a septuagenarian general manager and a coach who treats losing like he's biting down on a leather strap—and a goalie, now—the question is, how high, how fast?

"Well, you guys ask me that every three weeks," Babcock said. "We like to speed it up as fast as we possibly can. Getting good players helps you get better. He's a kid, though. I don't know how long it's going to take. You see lots of kids go lots of places around the league. And to me, if you surround them with some good veterans, you have a chance."

But the search for 30th is over now. Matthews was the end of that. Now comes what's next.

"You know, that's really up to them, when we go out on the ice and we start playing," Shanahan said. "It's up to how people come together, what kind of an off-season our guys have, and how quickly people gel. While it's a very compelling

and interesting question as to where are we in the upward trajectory, what's more important to us is, we have an upward trajectory.

"We said it last year: we wanted to become a team that could have success and be sustainable. And where we are in that timeline...we'll win a few games and people will say we're ahead, and we'll lose a few games and people will say we're not. It doesn't matter to me as much as whether we're moving forward, and whether we're moving towards the ultimate goal, which is to become a championship organization.

"We're just trying to get better. People need to understand that if we go out and get a player that would fit into that plan, we're not scrapping the plan, we're actually following the plan. What we're doing is chasing the vision. (Drafting Matthews is) incredibly significant. We see it as an important piece, but hockey's a team game, you need to surround people with other people.

"But tonight we get a very important piece, a centrepiece, to this young core of guys that we're putting together."

Auston Matthews may never be the captain of the Toronto Maple Leafs; Morgan Rielly may get there first. But he will feel the pressure Sundin felt, and maybe the adulation, too. He will be an 18-year-old hero in a city starved for a hockey team that doesn't embarrass it, or break its heart. The task is mammoth, for all of them.

"We appreciate that people like what we're doing, but we understand how far away we still are, "Shanahan said. "Even though you can say that when you're building a house that you laid a beautiful foundation, but there's still no walls, you're still not living in it. There's no roaring fire. You haven't built a great house yet: you've maybe done the first steps."

The first steps are complete. The climb, wherever it leads, starts now. ●

The Maple Leafs hope to build a contender around top draft pick Auston Matthews. (Carlos Osorio/Toronto Star)

Gone but Fondly Remembered

Looking back at the lives of eight men who played instrumental roles in the development and growth of the Toronto Maple Leafs as players, coaches and executives.

Conn Smythe (1895-1980)

Dick Darrell/Toronto Star

Constantine Falkland Cary "Conn" Smythe, the man who built Maple Leaf Gardens and made the Maple Leafs Canada's hockey team, died yesterday at his Toronto home. He was 85.

More than anyone else, Smythe elevated the status of hockey in Canada, turning Saturday night hockey at the Gardens into a social event, a super-colossal spectacle, part of Canadian culture now for half a century.

When he took control of the franchise in the mid-1920s, attendance at pro hockey on many occasions could be counted in hundreds. Before he left the hockey scene in the 1960s, there hadn't been an empty seat in the Gardens in almost two decades, and there still isn't.

Smythe sold control of the Gardens in 1961 to his son Stafford, Harold Ballard, who now controls the building, and John W.H. Bassett, chairman of Baton Broadcasting Inc. He remained a director until 1965.

In recent years, Smythe's name was more recognizable at the racetrack than in the hockey arena. His racing interests were among the country's most prominent and two of his horses won the Queen's Plate.

He had a distinguished military career, carried his fighting instinct into battle in two conflicts, was a prisoner of war, was wounded and was decorated.

To Smythe, hockey—like life—was a battle.

"If you can't lick 'em in the alley, you can't beat 'em on the ice," he told his players. He meant it. It was his philosophy in one sentence.

From the archives of the Toronto Star, November 19, 1980

Hap Day (1901-1990)

Nat Turofsky/HHOF Images

When he made his last appearance at the Gardens, for the ceremonial faceoff of the 1988-89 season, Hap Day looked so lean and hardy that long-time friends and admirers charged him with trying to parlay his famous rigid discipline and clean living into immortality.

Hap did well at it. He was 88 when he passed away peacefully in St. Thomas, Ont., yesterday.

It was Conn Smythe who persuaded Day into accepting a career in professional hockey, instead of his intended profession as a pharmacist. Within a year, Smythe bought the Toronto St. Pats and changed the name to the Maple Leafs.

Day launched his career on the night of Nov. 13, 1924, as a left winger. As soon as Smythe took over, he switched the young druggist to the blue line.

As a coach, Day was the first in the NHL to win the Stanley Cup in three successive seasons (1946-49). He also was the only coach to lose the first three games of a seven-game Stanley Cup final and still win the series.

That happened in 1942, when he made a roster switch which earned a footnote in hockey folklore by benching Gord Drillon and Bucko McDonald, two of his established stars, for two younger players, Don Metz and Ernie Dickens.

When the Leafs won the next four games, the lineup switch was seen as the reason for the turnaround.

By Milt Dunnell, February 18, 1990

Harold Ballard (1903-1990)

Harold Edwin Ballard, 86, is dead, although around Maple Leaf Gardens they're not sure. They're waiting for more evidence. There were no earthquakes, no explosions, no fireworks. They doubt he would have gone that quietly.

Boris Spremo/Toronto Star

Ballard, majority owner of Maple Leaf Gardens, had been in poor health for several years but until recently he was able to pretend he didn't notice. He did everything he wanted to do. It just took him a little longer.

Now that he's gone they're calling him a legend, but that's just one of the things they're calling him.

Other tributes are stupid, smart, treacherous, loyal, cruel, kind, a sinner, a saint, a bully, a softie, outrageous, compassionate; a grandstander bent on self-aggrandizement; a blasphemer publicly, a believer privately; a sentimental old fool, a selfish old slob—you name it.

He used to say with a mocking, belly-shaking laugh, that all of those descriptions fit; then he would add: "I don't give a good (deleted) what anybody says."

He did, though, and he would resolve to be more careful and diplomatic the next time. Then he would say, or do, something even more outlandish.

Call him a miserable old bastard, which many did, and he would beam approvingly. Remind him of a charitable act and he would feel uncomfortable.

"There's no such thing as a nice guy, " he would say. "Mr. Nice Guys are all fakes."

By Rex MacLeod, April 12, 1990

Turk Broda (1914-1972)

Turk Broda, hockey's beloved Fat Man, died last night of a heart attack. He was 58.

In his day, as the Toronto Maple Leaf all-star goalie, Broda was renowned as the finest of all National Hockey League players whenever the pressure was great and the games were extra important. Two of his

Nat Turofsky/HHOF Images

records still stand: 13 playoff shutouts and 101 Stanley Cup matches, and he twice won the Vezina Trophy as the league's top goalie.

Over his 14-year career—interrupted by a two-year wartime hitches in the Canadian army—his goals-against average improved by half a goal whenever he faced the tension of Stanley Cup competition.

Asked one time to explain this knack of his, he replied, "I always needed the money."

Broda's stature as one of the best goalies ever to play in the NHL is unquestioned, but hockey fans will also remember him as one of the most popular personalities of his era, a perpetually cheerful man whose shortcomings were not much different from those of the average man, and they'll remember his own battle of the bulge.

After his playing career, Broda went into coaching and was a tremendously successful one, winning five Ontario junior championships with Marlboro B and A teams, as well as two Canadian titles.

He handled professionals from time to time, too, but his greatest achievements were with juniors and the future big-leaguers he coached included Billy Harris, Bob Pulford, Bob Baun, Al MacNeil, Carl Brewer, Garry Unger and Jim Dorey.

He was elected to hockey's Hall of Fame in 1967 with marvelous credentials—five Stanley Cup victories, his two Vezina trophies and three all-star nominations.

Broda spent almost his entire life in hockey but he had no connection with the game when he died. Hockey did not leave him financially secure. The same talent today would make a man a millionaire.

By Jim Proudfoot, October 18, 1972

Ted (Teeder) Kennedy (1925-2009)

Nat Turofsky/HHOF Images

Ted (Teeder) Kennedy, who died of heart failure yesterday at 83 in a Port Colborne nursing home, was a Leaf centre for 12 seasons. He was part of five Stanley Cup victories; was team captain from 1948 to '57 and was the last Leaf to win the Hart Trophy as the NHL's most valuable player, in 1955.

Former teammate Dick Duff said Kennedy was the perfect Leaf captain, embodying the qualities of determination and tenacity along with a relentless will to succeed.

"He showed pride in Toronto, pride in the Leafs and always tried to find ways to win, " Duff told the Star's Paul Hunter. "If someone was writing a book about Toronto and the Leafs and what the team meant to the city, the biggest chapter would be on Kennedy."

Kennedy's hockey success came through hard work. He was not an easy skater, appearing to run, not glide, on the blades, often with a look on his face as if he were in pain, perspiring from the effort. To compensate for his lack of speed, Kennedy carefully honed his other skills, especially passing the puck.

He was a master at using the players on the ice with him, notably wingers Howie Meeker and Vic Lynn, and most hockey old-timers regard him as the best at winning faceoffs.

"I never had much speed...so I compensated by using my wingers," Kennedy said. "To be able to pass reasonably well made up for my lack of speed."

By Frank Orr, August 15, 2009

Steve Stavro (1926-2006)

When it came to sports, Steve Stavro possessed a keen sense of anticipation and optimism. It's a trait common to those involved in horse racing; some say it keeps them young.

Boris Spremo/Toronto Star

Stavro was better known—regrettably famous and almost infamous—for owning the Maple Leafs for a contentious decade or so and he and the fans in this city dreamed the big dreams there, too. They went unmet on his watch, although that certainly didn't make him unique.

Stavro, who died of a heart attack on Sunday, aged 78, was a guy who grew up the hard way. Worked hard. Got up early in the morning and kept his hands on his businesses.

When it came to sports, he was an owner in the old-fashioned sense of the word, which means he was different from the mere investors and money lenders who in 2002 squeezed him out of what is now Maple Leaf Sports and Entertainment.

He thought players made too much money and rejected the chance to add Wayne Gretzky late in his career as being too expensive.

He didn't know how to begin to deal with the Maple Leaf Gardens pedophilia scandal, a messy affair he inherited, along with the hockey team.

He had his enemies—who doesn't?—but he made himself a lot of friends in soccer, horse racing, junior hockey, around the Leafs. One of a kind? No question. No one else like him in this town.

By Dave Perkins, April 25, 2005

Tim Horton (1930-1974)

Nat Turofsky/HHOF Images

Punch Imlach says that while he was the architect of Maple Leafs' great Stanley Cup winning teams of the 1960s, Tim Horton, who met an untimely death in a car crash on the Queen Elizabeth highway yesterday, was the ice-general who made it all possible.

"I think Horton, more than any other one player, was the key to those glory days," said the former Leaf coach who is general manager of Buffalo Sabres.

"He had lost a little speed since then, but in our smaller rink was doing the same job for Buffalo Sabres. He rates with Eddie Shore, Doug Harvey, Bobby Orr and other all-time National Hockey League defence greats."

Horton played 22 seasons in the toughest league in hockey without dishing out a mean or vicious blow.

The reason this is so startling is that the 44-year-old Horton was endowed with almost superhuman physical strength. National Hockey League president Clarence Campbell praised Horton for the cleanness of his play.

Leaf coach Red Kelly said: "I'd like to have 18 Hortons on a team. I played against him for 7½ seasons when I was in Detroit. I found him one of the toughest dang guys to beat in the league and, when he got you in the corner that was it."

"A dreadful shock because of its suddenness," said Leaf captain Dave Keon. "He was a great player, a great person and a close friend. What more can I say that hasn't been said?"

By Red Burnett, February 22, 1974

Pat Quinn (1943-2014)

Rene Johnston/Toronto Star

Former Leafs coach and GM Pat Quinn, who wanted to become a priest until the game took him in another direction, has died, aged 71.

Quinn was an old-school NHL defenceman but he was also unconventional, obtaining a law degree after retiring as a player—unprecedented at the time—so that he could understand contracts as a future NHL executive.

A smart cookie, not a cement head. His post-game press conferences were often hockey tutorials for journalists. Few could explain the game as well as Quinn.

He was the last of the old two-hats—coach-GM—during his stint in Toronto from 1998 to 2006, until essentially replacing himself in the latter position with John Ferguson Jr. in 2003, purportedly to prevent Dryden from hiring his preferred candidate, Bob Gainey.

Twice a Jack Adams Award winner—in Philadelphia and Vancouver—as coach of the year, Quinn liked his teams jumbo-sized and rough-hewn, like him, but he deeply appreciated skill—marquee studs Pavel Bure with the Canucks and Mats Sundin with the Leafs.

"Pat was a father figure and a great person," Sundin told the Star on Monday from Sweden. "The biggest lesson I learned from Pat was to take responsibility for my play on the ice, but also take responsibility for my life. Pat said: 'Hockey is a great way to find out whom you are, whom you want to be and what you are made of.'"

By Rosie DiManno, November 25, 2014

The Future

Shanahan Finds Leafs' Potential Saviour.
The Question Is Whether Ownership Will Stick to the Plan

By Damien Cox

It was a demonstration that even as a master recruiter—the man who convinced Mike Babcock to come to Toronto as head coach when absolutely nobody in the hockey world thought he could—Brendan Shanahan doesn't always get his way.

For years, the Maple Leaf organization had looked forward to the summer of 2016 as the summer they'd be able to pursue and land Steven Stamkos, not just one of the NHL's premier snipers but a Toronto area boy to boot.

Even in good times over the past 50 years—and, really, before that— the Leafs have almost never had a local lad leading the way.

Syl Apps was from Paris, Ont. and Ted Kennedy was from the Lake Erie town of Port Colborne. George Armstrong was from Sudbury, Dave Keon from Noranda, Que. Darryl Sitter was born in St. Jacobs, Rick Vaive, the star of the hopeless 1980s, hailed from Ottawa. Mats Sundin was from Bromma, Sweden, Doug Gilmour was from Kingston.

Not since the pre-World War II days when Toronto's own Charlie Conacher scored so many important goals, have the Leafs had a local player of such prominence. For years, the modern Leafs dreamed of the possibility Stamkos could be that player.

But then, abruptly, just hours before hitting the market as an unrestricted free agent on July 1, Stamkos signed an eight-year contract to stay with the Tampa Bay Lightning.

Dream dead. Just like that.

Except it didn't really go over that way. Sure, on social media, some interpreted Stamkos' decision as a massive snub, a repudiation of the Leafs efforts to become competitive again. Sarcastic types suggested the Leafs could now shift their focus to stealing the star of another team, such as New York Islanders centre John Tavares when he becomes a free agent in 2018.

But the larger reaction seemed to be something like, well, too bad, but onward and upward. Just days earlier, after all, the Leafs had drafted Auston Matthews with the first over-all pick of the 2016 NHL draft.

Shanahan had already found his potential saviour and, at least for now, at a much more affordable price.

The Leafs had never owned Stamkos, so most seemed to understand they hadn't lost anything when he decided to stay with the Lightning. This wasn't a step back in this massive rebuilding program. It just wasn't a big step forward.

More importantly, the Leaf organization didn't react to the lost opportunity to court Stamkos by throwing millions of dollars at lesser free agents such as Milan Lucic, Andrew Ladd or David Backes.

They did give former Islander winger Matt Martin a four-year contract worth $2.5 million per season, a healthy raise for the league's No. 1 hitter, but hardly an albatross-like contract if it doesn't work out.

Mitch Marner, take fourth over-all in the 2015 draft, is a key building block for the future. (Carlos Osorio/Toronto Star)

They also brought back defenceman Roman Polak on a one-year deal for $2.25 million after dealing Polak to San Jose at the trade deadline to be part of the Sharks' run to the Stanley Cup final.

And that was it. In other words, after missing out on Stamkos, the Leafs got back to the plodding business of slowly building a champion, which—should it prove successful—will be primarily about drafting the right players and developing them the right way.

In the final analysis, that's what this will be about: the ability of an organization that has rarely been able to stay focused over the past 50 years on the ultimate prize to stay focused this time around.

The question isn't, "Will the Leafs eventually win the Stanley Cup?"

It's, "Will the Leafs stick to a plan that may give them the opportunity to compete for a Stanley Cup?"

That's all you can really try to do in a 30-team league. Teams such as St. Louis, Washington and San Jose showed again in the '16 Stanley Cup playoffs that seemingly doing all the right things for years and years may not lead to drinking champagne out of the most beautiful trophy in sports.

In Matthews, the Leafs have that major piece to build around, just as Edmonton has with Connor McDavid and Buffalo with Jack Eichel; just as Pittsburgh in 2005 landed Sidney Crosby, who delivered a second Cup to that city this spring.

The Scottsdale-born Matthews joins Mitch Marner, William Nylander and other young hopefuls as the future of the team and Frederik Anderson has supplanted Jonathan Bernier as the new starting goalie.

Martin and Polak complement a group of 2016 draftees who seem more about size and muscle than the pure skill the team had focused on the year before. That suggests there's an effort to develop a team along the lines of the three-time champions from Chicago—they're capable of playing the game any way you want to play it.

There many variables that will determine whether this all leads somewhere, so it is impossible to actually determine the quality of the Toronto rebuild at this point. Certainly, if Matthews doesn't turn out to be a star, that will be a massive step backwards in the way not getting to bid on Stamkos was not.

In the short term, as young players get NHL opportunities they wouldn't get with contending clubs, it's quite conceivable the Leafs may continue to lose more games than they win and stumble about in the league basement.

For this to turn out differently than rebuilds of the past, either the short-lived ones or those that never really got off the ground, the key will the way in which ownership reacts, how Shanahan and the hockey department reacts.

For a century, it has been a challenge to build a champion in a city that deeply loves the sport and is populated by tens of thousands of armchair quarterbacks. It's a challenge that was met by Conn Smythe and Punch Imlach and, to lesser degrees, by Steve Stavro and Pat Quinn.

In a hockey world that grows more complicated, not less, and more competitive, not less, that challenge is exponentially more difficult than it was the day Smythe opened the doors to Maple Leaf Gardens.

Players, as Stamkos demonstrated, have more say and more personal wealth today than Smythe could ever have imagined and, as the league expands again, this time to Las Vegas for the 2017-18 season, the number of towns chasing the Cup continues to grow.

One hundred years after beginning as the Toronto Arenas, and then becoming the St. Patricks before evolving into the Maple Leafs, Toronto has 13 Stanley Cups to its credit, but none since 1967.

The hope is that Matthews will lead the way to the next one. Son of an American father and a Mexican mother who grew up in Arizona and played his draft season in Switzerland, he represents the internationalism and variety of the modern game and over-all hockey culture.

For the first time since the club was founded, the Leafs appear to be on the cutting edge of hockey history. This will be a fascinating ride to watch and experience. ●